Anything But Silent

Mark Drolsbaugh

Anything But Silent

Published by: Handwave Publications
1121 Bethlehem Pike, # 60-134
Springhouse, PA 19477

ISBN: 0-9657460-3-8

Library of Congress Control Number: 2003109094

Dedicated to Rachel Paul, Dottie Leonard, Roy Farrar, Tom Scattergood, Mally Cox-Chapman, Joan Coale, David Sanders, and Peter Reinke. Thank you for teaching thousands of kids, including a very strange deaf one, to appreciate the joys of writing.

Acknowledgements

To Melanie, Darren, and Brandon, for tolerating thousands of *"just one more minute, I'm almost done."*

To my parents and grandparents, whose love and support is an inspiration.

To Dr. I. King Jordan, for graciously agreeing to write the Foreword. When Dr. Jordan became the first deaf president of Gallaudet University, it inspired me to transfer to Gallaudet. Without Gallaudet, this book doesn't happen.

To Trudy Suggs of T.S. Writing Services. She has this Midas touch that never ceases to amaze me. Any organization or project she gets involved with significantly improves thanks to her endless creativity, dedication, and professionalism.

To Chuck and Yvonne Vermillion of Magic Graphix. Their expertise in layout and editing was a tremendous help in getting this book published.

To all of the staff and fellow writers at *DeafNation*, *Silent News*, *NAD Members Only Area*, and *SIGNews*. You rock.

To Damara Goff Paris. Her humor and insight kept me going as we learned to navigate the wild waters of the publishing business.

To MaryAnne Kowalczyk of Parents for Deaf Awareness. Through her tireless advocacy, MaryAnne ensures that parents of deaf children are well-informed and empowered.

To Carol Finkle and Creative Access, for connecting deaf and hearing audiences via the most magical moments in accessible entertainment.

To Jeff Jones, Vijay Advani, Jason McKinnie, and Derek Gambrell. We're still The Family.

To everyone at the Pennsylvania School for the Deaf. Thanks especially to Lisa Santomen, Sam Scott, and Stephanie Smith for always encouraging me to go after my dreams.

Table of Contents

Foreword

Reading is something I really love to do. The books I like to read are the ones that make me laugh or make me think. It's not very often that I read something that makes me do both. Mark Drolsbaugh's *Anything But Silent* is one of those rare books. As I was reading this book, I realized my eyes were just sliding across the page and I'd often find myself chuckling out loud. I often would catch myself thinking, hey, Mark's really got something there. He is saying something important!

Anything But Silent takes the reader on a journey into the rich tapestry that comprises the Deaf community. Mark Drolsbaugh demonstrates the many ways one can be deaf in the world and through his use of humor, the reader is able to understand what it essentially means to be a deaf person. Some people have told me they don't read often because they don't enjoy it. This book is so chock full of interesting things that even people who "don't like to read" will enjoy it.

Anything But Silent is a book I will recommend to my family and friends because it is definitely worth reading. I would also recommend this book for use in the classroom, especially with deaf students. It is a book that will spur debate among those who read it. Enjoy!

—*Dr. I. King Jordan*

Introduction

The way Mark and I met was somewhat odd, at least back in those days. Mark and I attended Gallaudet University at the same time, although he was a few years ahead of me. During the early 1990s, Gallaudet had what was called the VAX system—which was much like today's message boards on the web. People posted messages in discussion forums, and more often than not, these messages were off-the-wall and absolutely unrelated to the discussion; yet others were in-depth and excellent writings.

Mark's messages always made me chuckle in agreement with his candid perspectives, so I started asking around about who 11MDROLSBAUGH was. When I finally met him, I was impressed; he was actually as funny in person as he was online, and so genuine.

I have to admit, though, that when I met Mark, I immediately assumed he was from a hearing background, given his signing. His signing was good, but it wasn't at a level that a native signer would be. I was taken aback when I found out he actually was from a deaf family. Generally, deaf people who have deaf parents have a unique fluency of American Sign Language, much like a native speaker of Spanish achieves unique fluency.

But as I got to know Mark, I came to

realize the distinctive upbringing he had. It's quite unusual to see deaf parents who choose oral education for their deaf children, especially if the parents themselves went through the struggles of oralism. It's even more fascinating for me to see how Mark has returned to the deaf community and ASL, even though he wasn't really immersed in it during his childhood.

Mark and I have a lot in common. We both have deaf parents; we both attended public schools; we both are part of the rich Deaf culture and its nuances; we both work within the deaf community; we both write; and we both have very similar views about the world. Yet we didn't really become friends until after college, when our writing careers crossed paths.

Upon graduation from Gallaudet, I began writing for the now-defunct *DeafNation*, a newspaper within the deaf community. It was at the newspaper that I discovered Mark's brilliant, hilarious writing style. Whenever I got my copies of the newspaper, I'd quickly open up to his column (after checking my own articles, of course).

Eventually, when I became Editor in Chief of a competing newspaper, *Silent News*, I immediately made Mark a regular columnist. His upfront, unpretentious observations of life as it is for a deaf person were always popular with readers. His observations were always on target. The reason Mark's work continues to be so popular with readers is because he's refreshing, funny, and *honest*.

You may be new to the deaf community, whether you're a parent, learning ASL, have a friend or relative who's deaf, or are simply curious about the deaf community. You'll encounter a lot of terms that are new ("oral?!" "hearing?!"). No matter how new you are to the community, you'll feel a sense of familiarity throughout Mark's articles, because he writes as if he's talking to *you.* You become drawn in, and end up feeling as if he's been part of your family forever.

I also hope that you will feel a sense of disbelief at how people could be so ridiculous or insensitive. You'll read about some individuals involved in seemingly outrageous behavior in *Anything But Silent,* and encounter issues that you may struggle with. But it's important that you develop an understanding and respect of why many culturally Deaf people actually appreciate and love being deaf.

If you're a deaf person reading this book, then you'll know all too well that the incidents Mark writes about really do take place. The sheer madness of the experiences Mark describes is what makes the reader laugh, especially with his take on them. Yet we need to remember that these real-life incidents can make a major impact upon the child who has very little in terms of deaf role models or identity.

Anything But Silent is an excellent overview of experiences in a deaf man's life. It's my hope that you will enjoy this book as much as I did. And reread it. And share the book with others. I'm proud to have been part of Mark's journey from college frat boy to accomplished writer.

Trudy Suggs
Faribault, MN

Anything But Silent

I've been wondering about the use of the word "silent" throughout deaf history. It's a word that goes back a long way. Several deaf clubs have used it. The Metro Silent Club and the Silent Athletic Club, for example. It has always baffled me. Because as far as I can tell, nothing in the deaf world is silent.

Before anyone howls in protest, let's look at the evidence. First, let's go back to the early '70s, to a brisk evening in Atlantic City. I was seven or eight years old at the time, walking down the street with my family. We're a mixed bag, my family. Some of us deaf, some of us hearing.

As it so happened, a deaf woman walked down the other side of the street and noticed us. She needed directions but wasn't sure how to ask. One second someone in our group was signing, and then all of a sudden everyone was using voice. This mystery woman got confused and didn't know how to approach us.

She walked up, hesitated, and then started to sign. She quickly changed her mind and switched to voice, then went back to signing. Suddenly she changed her mind once more

1

and just yelled at us in the loudest voice I'd ever heard: "WHERE IS THE BOARDWALK?!?!" The boardwalk was one block behind her, glittering lights and all. This woman was definitely not silent, and definitely not sober.

This exchange took only thirty seconds but my father milked it for years. Countless times he'd startle me out of my shoes by suddenly yelling, "WHERE IS THE BOARDWALK?!?!" My parents may be deaf, but they sure aren't silent.

Jumping ahead to the late '80s, trust me when I say that many of my deaf friends were as caught up in the Michael Jackson and MC Hammer craze as any hearing folks. Again, not silent.

Back then I got a job as dorm counselor at the Pennsylvania School for the Deaf. Most of my ear-shattering memories involve the basketball team. Whether it was all pandemonium breaking loose after a game-winning shot or the crowd stomping its feet to distract an opponent at the free throw line, the noise level shook the roof.

After not finding any silence at PSD, I became a member of the, ahem, Silent Athletic Club in Northeast Philadelphia. My first impression there was the loud, thumping, ground-shaking, heart-pounding music. And that was just in the parking lot where some guy in a white Camaro had his stereo turned up full blast.

Inside the actual club itself, a nuclear-powered jukebox rocked the building so hard it registered on the Richter scale. Any residual hearing I had left was now gone and thus I was eligible to enroll at Gallaudet University—where once again, I failed miserably in my search for silence.

At Gallaudet, I quickly learned that Spirit Week,

Rockfest, NTID/Gally Weekend, and plenty other events made the Silent Athletic Club seem like a convent. Dorm parties, too. I'll never forget the guy who hooked up his TV and VCR to a pair of gargantuan speakers. He blew out what was left of my eardrums with a ridiculously loud showing of the Arnold Schwarzenegger movie *Total Recall.* I totally recall having tinnitus for a week. Fun? Oh yeah. Silent? Not by a long shot.

Now take the cumulative noise of Atlantic City, PSD, SAC, and Gallaudet. Multiply it by ten and you get the current noise level in my house. Yes, I have two kids. I can't hear myself think.

That's it. I've called off the search. There is no silence in the deaf community. We party, we stomp our feet, and we scream with the best of them. But if you want to use the word "silent," that's fine. I kind of like it, irony and all. Despite our inherent loudness, "silent" is a big part of our legacy, something we've put in our history books for future generations to appreciate.

Accurate or not, be proud of our "silent" heritage. Just find the boardwalk yourself and keep that stereo away from me.

I Hate Cold Cuts

"**S**ixteen! Sixteen... sixteen? Okay, seventeen!" A middle-aged lady brushed past me and made her way to the counter. By the time I realized what happened, it was too late. Too late to trip her with a banana peel, forearm smash, or a flying piledriver. Mrs. Seventeen had me beat. Yes, I was the pathetic schmuck holding ticket stub number sixteen.

Don't you just hate the deli counter at the supermarket? I know I do. So does my wife, which is why she takes great pleasure in making me stand in line for honey maple, uh, glazed maple, uh, honey glazed, ham maple banana turkey ham, whatever it is she sends me there for.

First of all, cold cuts aren't good for you. Doesn't anyone know what processed meat is? It's something like five percent turkey, five percent Alpo, five percent Meow Mix, and eighty-five percent toxic waste.

On top of that, my male ego hates standing in line. Yes, the same male ego that won't let me stop the car and ask for directions. My

Inner Neanderthal finds it absolutely repulsive to stand there and be at the mercy of some strange guy calling numbers. I prefer to roar down the supermarket aisles at top speed, thumping my chest, haphazardly dumping all sorts of goodies in the cart. Then I zoom through the express checkout line even if I have six thousand items in my cart. I'm in, I'm out, bada-bing, bada-boom. Coupons? Nah. No time for them. One second I'm here, the next second I'm off to my next conquest. Ooga!

So to just stop and stand there, vacant look on my face, waiting for number sixteen to be called... I can't take it. I look around and I don't see people, I see domesticated poofsters. Poofsters standing obediently, tongues hanging out, tails wagging, waiting for the Alpha Male to call their number. Then they jump through a hoop and trample over the deaf guy who didn't hear number sixteen.

Oh yes, the deaf guy. What do we do about the deaf guy? Neanderthal or not, you have to agree that waiting for your number to be called is no enjoyable task when you're deaf. My neck is two inches longer from craning every which way as I try to keep my eye on the meat slicer. Then he goes ahead and quickly calls another number, which of course I miss. How's a deaf guy to keep up with this? How do we make this more deaf-friendly?

Maybe, with state of the art technology, we could have the ticket stubs programmed to self-destruct five seconds after their number is called, a la Mission Impossible. When your stub goes POOF in your hand, you know it's your turn. Then again, if you make the mistake of putting the stub in your pocket, you might give the other customers a neat show: you running down the aisles, pants on fire.

Know what I'd like? Add a computer to the ticket stub dispenser. Deaf customers could then type in special instructions such as "Customer is deaf; go crazy getting his attention." Once the deaf customer's number is called, lights flash all over the store. Confetti drops from the ceiling, fireworks go off, a disco ball twirls, and the Radio City Rockettes do a dance number on the counter. Cost-effective? Heck, no. Entertaining? Oh, yeah.

A cheaper method would be for stores to hire Tonya Harding. They call your number, you don't hear it, and then Tonya comes after you with a... oh, never mind. Scrap that.

The best solution, in my opinion, would be for stores to allow customers to pre-order their road kill, uh, cold cuts, via computer. This could be done with a computer in the store or even from the comfort of your own home. By the time you get to the counter, your order is ready. And to soothe my male ego, I'd add instructions that the meat slicer is to hike the package to a stock clerk, who laterals it to the store manager, who tosses a thirty-yard pass to me over at the checkout counter. The cashier would signal touchdown, I'd spike the meat, pay for it, and be on my way. Wifey gets her lunch and my dignity remains intact. I think.

All right. What really happened was I had no choice but to leapfrog over Mrs. Eighteen. I told the meat slicer I couldn't hear and that I didn't realize my number had been called until he already began serving Mrs. Seventeen. Mrs. Eighteen, thankfully, was a delightful woman who saw the whole thing and graciously allowed me to cut through.

The only sane suggestion I can make is to remind the meat slicer you're deaf and politely suggest that he consistently update the numbers on the screen as he calls them out (the guy at my store was calling sixteen and seventeen while the screen remained stuck on eleven).

Or, simply show this article to the folks at the supermarket and give them a nice laugh. They may or may not accommodate you with the Rockettes, but they'll remember who you are and serve you better the next time.

Editor's note: A year after this article was first published, several stores in Mark's hometown actually installed computers where you can type in your order for the deli and pick it up after you finish shopping. Although there is no evidence of any connection, Mark hasn't stopped bragging that his incredibly powerful article has revolutionized the entire supermarket industry.

We've Come a Long Way, But...

*O*ne of my favorite poems of all time is Willard Madsen's *You Have to be Deaf to Understand*. I'm not really that much of a poetry nut but this one really strikes home. There have simply been too many incidents where I was left wondering if deaf people would ever be truly understood. Examples of such incidents are:

- A deaf woman requests an interpreter for a traffic court hearing. She gets the interpreter and wins her case, but afterwards she is confronted by the policeman who ticketed her. Shaking his head disapprovingly, the officer says, "You know, you should learn how to read lips."

- A deaf patron can't understand the waiter at a restaurant. He mentions that he's deaf. The waiter goes, "Oh, I'm sorry..." and then proceeds to yell in the deaf customer's ear.

- The only deaf person in a large family sits bored out of his mind while hearing relatives (who don't sign) chatter for several hours. When he finally can't tolerate the boredom anymore, he politely excuses himself. Immediately, family members protest and insist he should stay.

- A parent at a deaf social event meets a hard of hearing girl who has relatively good speech. In front of her prelingually deaf child, she approaches the girl and says, "Oh, you speak so well!" She turns to her own child and says, "See, if you study hard, you can speak like she can." The parent then looks for her child's teacher and asks her why she isn't teaching her child how to speak "like that wonderful girl over there."

- A deaf woman is attending an event with her family, which is a mix of both hearing and deaf people. She is sharing stories of famous deaf embarrassing moments. Her favorite is the one where she inadvertently set off her car alarm and didn't realize it until after getting funny looks from her neighbors. While deaf relatives howl with laughter, the hearing folks aren't amused. In fact, the woman's hearing mother gets upset. She wonders out loud if a cochlear implant would have prevented the incident.

- This one has happened many times: A deaf person at an airport or bus terminal informs the attendant that he can't hear. Five minutes later, a wheelchair is rolled out for the deaf traveler.

Whether the above stories are amusing or disturbing, one thing remains clear: we need to continue advocating deaf awareness. Despite recent trends that have made the deaf community more visible (ADA, widespread availability of interpreters, captioned TV, assistive devices, community events, etc), it doesn't necessarily mean people understand who we are and what we're about. As I've pointed out in past articles, there are so many variations of deafness. We're a mixed bag. We're so diverse that Mr. Average Guy doesn't know what to make of us.

There are deaf people who sign fluently in ASL, American Sign Language. Then again, some might prefer PSE, Pidgin Signed English. There are so many other variations of sign language that I need a scorecard to keep up with them.

Meanwhile, there are those who prefer oralism, all voice and no signing. But, waitaminute, there are also a lot of switch-hitters out there—deaf people who use any combination of sign and voice as they see fit.

You also have deaf people with varying degrees of deafness: totally deaf, hard of hearing, late-deafened, and so on. One deaf person may wear a hearing aid while another may choose not to. Some may have a cochlear implant. Some will insist they are "hearing impaired" while others say, "I'm deaf, period."

Ask any of the above where they went to school and you'll get a wide range of answers and opinions: residential schools, mainstream schools, signing programs, and oral programs. Ask them which is best and watch the sparks fly. It's not unusual at all to see deaf people vehemently disagreeing with each other on many deaf-related issues.

What with the many viewpoints of the hard of hearing, deaf, culturally Deaf, late-deafened or hearing, how do we really understand deafness?

Some ways we can help others understand deafness would be: by respecting each other as individuals, by recognizing how one size does not fit all, by truly socializing with and getting to know each other, and by encouraging each other to succeed through whatever means is best for each individual. We can celebrate our unique individuality, yet bond together as a strong community. Only then, with an open mind, can we truly understand and be understood.

Say What?

*E*very now and then I get a certain compliment from hearing people. Unbeknownst to them, it is simultaneously a blessing and a curse.

"Wow, you have such wonderful speech!"

For a deaf guy, yeah, I do. I'm postlingually deaf. I was born hearing, and then around age five or so my ability to hear took a nosedive. This pattern can be traced back three or so generations on my father's side of the family. We appear to be hearing for a while, and then we go deaf. If there is a plus side to postlingual deafness, it's acquisition of speech. If there is a negative side to postlingual deafness, it's... acquisition of speech.

Sure, intelligible speech can often be an advantage. There are times when I need to talk to hearing people and it comes in handy. Not many hearing people use sign language, after all. There are probably a lot of situations where my speech ability has helped me communicate with hearing people. I don't deny that. But there's also another side of the story. For all of the ability I have relaying spoken information to hearing people, I am still deaf. I still have tremendous difficulty *receiving* information from people who do not sign.

One of my favorite examples is the time my wife and I stopped at a local fast-food restaurant. After a hard day at work, we were both too pooped to cook a healthy dinner. We would have to settle for the coronary cheeseburger special accompanied by the usual grease fries.

Normally, ordering at a McDonald's or Burger King is not too hard for a deaf guy. The menu hasn't really changed that much over the last fifty years. On top of that most burger joints are deaf-friendly with picture menus where you can point to the meal of your choice.

However, one day my wife and I decided to add a little variety to our lives by stopping at an Arby's instead of the usual McDonald's or Burger King. Starved, I went ahead and ordered my meal while my wife wandered off to the ladies room. Immediately, I was stuck in a frustrating communication breakdown.

The guy behind the counter knew I was deaf as he saw me signing with my wife before I placed my order. He graciously spoke slower for me in an effort to help me lip-read. But once I used my voice, he switched back to speaking at normal speed. For whatever reason, he assumed that because I can speak, I must be able to hear better than the average deaf guy. Trust me; this is not true at all. In fact, my prelingually deaf wife hears more sounds than I do (okay, so she has a hearing aid; I haven't worn mine since I flushed it down the toilet in '78). Incidentally, my wife is also a much better lip reader than I am.

I was really bombing with this guy. I explained

that he still needed to speak slower, but didn't get anywhere even after he did. Apparently, Arby's has something like two or three versions of french fries. I did not know this and I was completely unprepared when the cashier asked me if I wanted the crispy curly version or the usual. I had no idea what he was talking about. There I was, using my allegedly wonderful speech, repeatedly going "Eh? Say what? Would I prefer what?" I was totally lost. It was easy for me to order at McDonald's because of my familiarity with their menu, but at Arby's I didn't stand a chance.

After several rounds of verbal volleyball, I finally had my fries. Exasperated, I turned around and noticed that my wife was already digging into her meal. She had gone ahead and ordered from another cashier. Apparently, she got what she wanted in a much shorter time frame. When I sat down at her table she shook her head and asked what took me so long.

"Geez, that cashier, I couldn't understand a word he..." I stopped in mid-sentence. Right then I noticed what made my wife such an effective communicator. There it was, sitting on the tray: a blue pen and a notepad. While I was yammering with the cashier, my wife quickly wrote her order on paper and got everything she wanted in a matter of seconds.

If there's a lesson to be learned here, it's this: whatever method you choose, remember that communication is a two-way street. Or, better yet, just stay home and cook your own danged meal.

Martial Arts:
The Door to "I Can"

*A*t first glance, we might seem a bit strange. After all, when you see a group of people cavorting in pajama-like clothes, you might think "mental hospital." Especially when we do weird things such as bowing, meditating, and twisting ourselves into human pretzels. Not to mention punching, kicking, tripping, grappling, and immobilizing each other with joint locks. Yes, we're martial artists. I love it.

Over the years, I've participated in a number of martial arts styles whenever time permitted. In between school, job changes, relocating to new neighborhoods, and raising two kids, I've been fortunate to be able to participate in Shotokan, Tae Kwon Do, Tai Chi, and Kempo.

You'd think that with two kids in the house it would be time to hang up the uniform and call it a career. After all, it's not easy to practice at home when your three-year-old frequently interrupts your workout with a football thrown at your crotch. But I've got kung fu fever and just can't stop.

Speaking of kids, that brings us to the main point of this article: why aren't there more deaf kids signing up for karate? They have everything in the world to gain from it and I highly recommend checking it out.

You've probably seen the karate ads in the phone book and rolled your eyes at all the gung-ho buzzwords: Confidence! Self-control! Concentration! Self-esteem! Respect! Discipline! Better grades! Lose Weight! Fix the kitchen sink!

Sounds hokey, sure, but they throw out those words for a reason: it's true. Want an example? Fine, let's start with confidence.

Many deaf kids are over-exposed to the worst four-letter word of them all: "can't." There are lots of people out there who feel that deaf kids are unable to succeed in the mainstream, and/or need to be protectively shielded from it. And "but you can't do that, you're deaf" is the worst message you can give a deaf child.

Unfortunately, children often internalize this "but you can't" mentality. They sense it from others, grow accustomed to it, and sooner or later start to believe it. They consequently go through life selling themselves short. They live down to the low expectations placed on them.

An excellent antidote for "but you can't", in my opinion, is the martial arts. A good karate school provides children with real-life experiences that clearly prove they can accomplish their goals.

When you participate in karate class as a beginner, you can't help but notice the advanced students performing all sorts of amazing physical feats. It's not unusual if you look at them and think, "No way could I ever do that." But after a certain period of time you WILL master those techniques. It comes with the program. Regular participation and an honest effort always bring results.

Inevitably, you reach a point where you're doing stuff you once thought was impossible. And that's when you reach the biggest mental breakthrough: "Hey, two years ago I said 'no way'—and now I'm doing it!" Once that realization sets in, you've established a foundation of confidence that allows you to go further and seek new challenges. You know firsthand that all it takes is perseverance and faith in yourself.

Another aspect you develop is concentration, an ability that can easily be transferred to school or the workplace. For me, this is the area where the martial arts help most. Look, I have a wife, two kids, a full time job, and a part time home business. With all that, who has time to think? People ask me about something I was supposed to do two days ago and I tell them I can't even remember what I did this morning. So what could I possibly do to maintain my sanity?

Yes, karate to the rescue again. Nothing works better at clearing the clutter out of a frazzled brain. For example, there are plenty of moves you have to memorize and practice constantly before they become automatic. There are plenty of techniques where your feet are doing one thing while your hands are doing another. Without proper focus and concentration, these moves won't fly. It's not just physical exercise, it's also brain exercise.

Not long ago, I had fun with this in a middle school math class. The kids had to kick a small target pad which they could only hit if they properly focused on the task at hand. Then they switched

17

gears and did two-minute math drills, once under normal circumstances and again in a setting where we tried to throw them off task with numerous distractions. Both times, they nailed it. They learned to focus.

All of this is just the tip of the iceberg. There are plenty of other mental, physical, and spiritual benefits that come with the martial arts, but there isn't enough time or space to cover them in just one article. To learn about them, you have to experience them. And I'll just close by reiterating the most important point: if you're looking for ways to empower yourself or your children, the answer may be no further than the karate school right down the street.

I Work With Problem Children... Or Do I?

*O*ver the years, I've had the pleasure of working or interning at five different schools serving deaf children. Among those five are three mainstream schools, a residential school, and a day school. At each one of them, I've encountered what you might call "problem children." You know, the ones who always seem to do the opposite of what you tell them to do. The ones who get labeled oppositional, immature, unable to pay attention, and so on. But sometimes I wonder if we are too quick to slap a label on these kids.

Don't get me wrong, I definitely know that there are kids who are correctly diagnosed with attention deficit hyperactivity disorder, learning disabilities, and so on. I've worked with some of them myself. I've also seen actual cases of schizophrenia, autism, and manic depression. Such cases are out of my league and are appropriately handled by qualified professionals. I've been fortunate to be able to observe some excellent therapists and it's been an incredible learning experience.

At the same time, there was an incident not long ago that left me thinking that maybe, just maybe, we might be giving some deaf kids a bum rap when we judge them to be problem children. For a good example of what I'm talking about, let's take a close look at an example I will refer to as Exhibit A.

During a recent science lecture, Exhibit A took a seat at the end of a large boardroom table. Way up front a guest speaker stood next to a small movie screen as she presented a slide show to the audience. Since the lecturer was hearing, an interpreter was brought in. Immediately, Exhibit A began squirming in his seat *(Uh-oh, inappropriate behavior)*. Not only was he frustrated at having to stare at the interpreter as the lecturer paced the room, but it so happened the interpreter was using SEE (Signing Exact English).

After ten minutes of trying to keep up with a difficult science topic presented entirely in SEE, Exhibit A became noticeably flustered. He spun around in his swivel chair and glanced around the room, all the while missing bits and pieces of the lecture *(Tsk, tsk... terribly inappropriate)*.

Exhibit A tried his best to follow the interpreter but his eyes ached too much. He blinked. He rubbed his eyes. He was out of it. He slipped his shoes off and dangled them off his toes *(Bad kid, not paying attention at all)*.

Twenty minutes later Exhibit A had a knot in his stomach. He couldn't take it anymore. He took a deep breath and shifted in his seat impatiently. He finally gave up and took a bathroom break that wasn't really necessary *(Hmm... maybe this kid has ADHD)*.

After a delightful excursion to the boys' room, Exhibit A was in no hurry to return to The Presentation from Hell. He took a long, unnecessary

20

detour around the building before returning to the lecture *(Tsk, tsk... delinquent behavior)*. Upon returning to the room, Exhibit A ignored the lecture and began to chat discreetly with another deaf person *(What a bad influence!)*.

This particular lecture had both hearing and deaf people present. Exhibit A noticed that it was mostly the hearing people who were participating in class discussion. Other deaf people seemed to be nodding off just as he did *(Hey kid, pay attention!)*.

Shrugging, Exhibit A blew off the group discussion and began to crack jokes with the deaf peer right next to him *(Deaf kids are just so difficult in the classroom, aren't they?)*.

Finally, when the lecture was over Exhibit A and his friend made a beeline to the buffet table and helped themselves to a free lunch *(Such immature, self-centered behavior!)*.

Exhibit A must be a classic example of the typical deaf problem child, right? Umm, I'm afraid not. After all, Exhibit A happens to be someone we know very well.

Yup, you saw this coming from a mile away. Yup, that was me squirming in the boardroom. It happened at a mental health professionals' workshop that had me wondering about the state of my own mental health. Either I'm a thirty-year-old problem child with ADHD or there's something else going on here. Yup, I believe it's a communication issue, not a behavior issue.

When challenging, new topics are presented, I absorb them much more efficiently when they are presented in ASL. I need *visual* stimulation. An interpreter is okay, more so when he or she uses ASL. But I can't stare at such a limited space for so long without the freedom to glance around. I'm only human and my eyes need a break. They literally go dry if I stare at an interpreter for more than half an hour. Meanwhile, hearing people can glance around all they want, take notes, and even close their eyes while absorbing information with their ears. Deaf people do not have this luxury.

On the other hand, I swear time flies in a group discussion where all the participants are using ASL. In such situations I've been able to hang in there for hours, glancing around and following a conversation going on in the most visually appealing and accessible language for me. That's just the way it is. ASL is a fresh, lively means of communication. It keeps me awake. With SEE, I have to reach for the Visine and I've often misunderstood a lot of things.

There are similar communication issues at home. When I'm with friends or relatives who use ASL, time flies in a group discussion. But with friends and relatives who do not sign, I have to put in an incredible effort to lip-read and use my speech. Not that I resent it, but the effort does indeed wear me out. I may either slip out and take a break or grit it out for the whole duration. Inevitably I wind up plopping on my couch in exhaustion by the end of the evening.

With this in mind, I understand all too well when deaf students show up for school in a cranky mood after spending the whole weekend with people who don't sign. I would also be restless and in dire need of stimulating communication.

All right, then. Maybe I am a problem child. Maybe I have ADHD. Maybe I'm a delinquent. But I really do believe I've stumbled on to an important point: if you have deaf children or if you're a teacher of deaf children, take a closer look if they're not behaving the way you'd like them to. In fact, take a closer look at *yourself* before you take a closer look at them. Are you communicating in the way most appropriate for their needs? Are you able to use ASL and support it with good use of facial expressions (if not, you might be signing in a monotone)? If your kids don't seem to understand your instructions, are you able to improvise and present information in a different way? Are you able to recognize which methods work best for each individual child?

It's not easy to do all this but I highly recommend it. For as guilty as I am of having ants in my pants, we all need to be careful before we stick our kids with the label of "problem child." After all, if we based all of our conclusions on first impressions, they would have hauled me out of that workshop in a straitjacket.

The Right to Know

While walking her class to the gym, PSD Teacher Aide Sherry Drolsbaugh (all right, so sue me for journalistic nepotism) noticed it was unusually windy. The kids, ranging in age from seven to nine, were struggling to walk straight in the blustery wind.

As the class approached the gym they crossed paths with maintenance man Joe Birdsall. Making a joking reference to the tornado movie *Twister*, Joe said it was so windy he saw a cow flying in the air. Sherry laughed and shook her head.

Some of the students caught the brief dialogue between the two deaf adults. They asked Sherry what was so funny. What did Joe say, they wanted to know. Did he really say that a cow just flew by?

Initially Sherry planned to say, "Yes, Joe made a silly joke," and then move on. But something gnawed at her. She thought about all the times, as a deaf child in a hearing family, that she had missed out on jokes and conversations. She remembered seeing a

relative crack a joke or two, watching her family
howl with laughter, and wanting so badly to know
what was going on. When she asked, all she could
get was:

> "Oh, your uncle just said something funny."
> "He made a joke... I'll tell you later."
> "He's talking about Johnny Carson."
> "He was... oh, never mind, finish your dinner."

Ouch! For many deaf people this is flashback
hell. Sherry realized that her students were in the
exact same boat as she once was in many years
ago. Adults were laughing and kids wanted to know
why. Acknowledging their right to know, Sherry
stopped in her tracks and repeated Joe's
wisecrack. As she explained that he said a cow
was flying in the wind, Joe approached them and
added that the cow made a very loud "moooooo"
as it flew over the school campus.

The kids ate it up. Apparently they connected it
with the Mother Goose nursery rhyme where the cow
jumps over the moon. They loved it. They asked
Sherry to tell the story again. They watched intently,
hanging on to every word. Some of the students got
excited and insisted a cow really did fly over the
school. Lively dialogue and a few mooooos
dominated the next several minutes.

During morning meeting the following day, the
kids insisted on telling the cow story all over again.
They all took turns describing the wind, the cow,
and the loud "moooooo" that could be heard all
over Philadelphia. They wrote the story down and
donated it to the school newsletter. Simply because
Sherry insisted on respecting their right to a

communicatively accessible environment, the kids had a wonderful experience.

As for our friend Elsie the Cow, she was last seen flying over Roosevelt Boulevard. Stay tuned to Deaf World TV for more news on the latest bovine sightings. After all, you have a right to know.

An ASL Perspective

When the Pennsylvania School for the Deaf hosted its second annual ASL Literature Contest, I was amazed once more. I thought the previous year's show was awesome, but this one absolutely rocked.

Sixty students participated in the contest. They had to present an ASL poem, skit, or story. Some of the students did the ever-popular ABC storytelling, where each sequential sign utilized a hand shape corresponding with the letters of the alphabet. Others signed amazingly creative stories using just one hand shape repeatedly throughout their routine. A few others made up dramatic vignettes about their favorite movies or superheroes. What with the many diverse routines, it was a fascinating show.

What really struck me, however, was the amount of confidence emanating from each student. We had grown accustomed to seeing many of them acting shy, withdrawn, and unwilling to be in the spotlight. As professionals, we often attribute this to language delays, inaccessible environments, communication problems at home, and so on. Yet with the ASL contest all of that dissipated. These kids were now on their home turf, standing on stage in front of a school wide audience, using the language they are most comfortable with. Basically, they got up there and kicked some major league butt.

One of the kids, who won first place in his age division, was a child who notoriously shuts down during educational or psychological evaluations. In my opinion, many of these so-called standard tests do nothing more than evaluate children from a white, hearing, American middle-class perspective. And this particular child, described by outside medical professionals as "shy" and "withdrawn", was standing there on stage making 150 people laugh with his prize-winning comedy routine. He did it in ASL, the language that allows him to show people what he's really made of.

The reason I bring this up is, quite obviously, the fact that we all need to be careful when we evaluate deaf children. In fact, not long ago I went through a confusing experience involving a new student's evaluation.

One of my duties as school counselor is to write social history reports for incoming students. I was halfway finished writing such a report on a four-year-old boy when I ran into a roadblock.

During the initial enrollment interview this boy was an angel. He was cooperative, playful, and demonstrated a wonderful sense of humor. As he went off to be evaluated by our staff, I continued interviewing this boy's mother to be sure I had all the information we needed. At one point in our discussion we were interrupted by a speech teacher, who simply had to tell the boy's mother what a great kid he was. The boy breezed through his evaluation and was an absolute joy to be with. Other evaluators, at one point or the other, echoed these sentiments. Obviously this was going to be an easy background report to write: *great kid, four-years-old, loves everybody, no problem, end of report.* It was a piece of cake until I stumbled onto his previous evaluation. In order to make sure I had the correct medical information I checked his previous file from another agency, and I was shocked at what I found. This very same kid was described as "impulsive," "withdrawn," and "not willing to socialize with others." Did I miss something somewhere? Was this boy kidnapped by aliens and replaced by a friendlier duplicate of himself? What happened?

I was frustrated. I was so sure I'd compiled an accurate report, and there I was holding a copy of a different report that said the exact opposite of everything I'd written. This needed to be cleared up fast. After checking and double-checking, the answer finally appeared. At the agency where they did the first evaluation, *no one used sign language.* Duh! Of course the kid didn't do what they asked. He didn't understand a word they said.

Troubled, I posted this topic on an Internet bulletin board and asked other deaf people for their feedback. The response was interesting. One person said a doctor once labeled him "anti-social" and "violent" because he couldn't understand the questions the doctor asked. Another person said that the psychological tests she took focused entirely on the hearing perspective. As she puts it, "all of the terms, questions, etc, represented hearing people... naturally, some of the things went off the chart because of this."

29

We really need to be careful in our assessment of deaf children. Yes, evaluations can be very important, but even more important are the evaluators themselves. Are they deaf-friendly? Do they sign? Are they able to accurately determine strengths and weaknesses? It's definitely something to keep in mind.

Several years ago, NBA superstar Michael Jordan abruptly retired from basketball and decided to try his luck at baseball. It was a valiant effort but he never made it to the big leagues. Several coaches commended his desire and perseverance but the truth was obvious: Jordan had joined baseball too late, he was too far behind, and in all likelihood he was a long shot to ever play for the Chicago White Sox.

Now suppose there was a baseball coach who didn't know anything about basketball. Suppose this coach had his head stuck so deep in the sand that he never knew who Michael Jordan actually was. At that point in time Jordan had already won three NBA championships and several MVP awards, and later he would win more. Nonetheless, suppose our hypothetical baseball coach was totally oblivious to all of Jordan's basketball exploits. Suppose this coach had to write an evaluation of Jordan's athletic skills. It would go something like this:

Great work ethic, but doesn't really understand the game. Started too late. Probably won't catch up. Can't hit the curve ball. Needs to focus on his footwork in the outfield. Doesn't understand the nuances of playing good defense. Very competitive, but this guy will never be a pro athlete.

You get my drift. You just don't ask a baseball guy to evaluate Michael Jordan as an athlete. For in the basketball world, he's considered one of the greatest superstars of all time. Likewise, with deaf children: if someone is evaluating them, that person needs to be aware of, and understand, the world of ASL and Deaf culture. For on stage that one day at PSD, we had sixty ASL versions of Michael Jordan drawing raucous rounds of applause.

ASL is a Bridge, Not a Barrier

*I*n August of 1997 I found myself smack in the middle of some controversial politics. At a local Intermediate Unit board meeting a decision was made that the county should consider adding a sign language program to what essentially had been an oral-only education for deaf children.

This was a unique experience for me because I got to see firsthand the impact parents can have on an education program. Basically, it was the parents, not the school board, who decided that the county should provide sign language instruction for its deaf students. Prior to the official board meeting, the parents had several meetings of their own to debate the issue. Further compounding the situation was the fact that the parents themselves were divided on whether or not they wanted sign language for their children.

Participating in the parent meetings were a number of deaf adults, myself included, who were asked to come and speak out on behalf of the virtues of sign language. We were invited to the meeting by parents who supported sign language and hoped that our input would influence the opposing parents.

One by one, a number of deaf people shared stories about sign language improving their lives in terms of accessibility, academic success, and overall happiness. It wasn't long before I noticed a great divide between opposing factions. I had the impression that some of the parents seemed to be afraid of Deaf culture, as if adding sign language would throw their children into an alien world where they would never be seen or heard from again.

This was where I saw an opening to express my own views. I jumped in on the discussion and pointed out that I originally went to a hearing school. As the only deaf student I was often frustrated and left out. I was isolated, an island unto myself. An island cut off from the joys of learning. Once my school hired a sign language interpreter, however, I had access to my education. I was able to stay at my school instead of flunking out. Sign language, then, helped me succeed in the hearing world. It did not alienate me from it.

Later on during the debate I remarked that I still have oral skills and I still use them. I could, I pointed out, have an oral discussion one-on-one with any of the hearing parents. However, without the services of the sign language interpreters who were working that night, I never would have been able to participate in the group meeting. Like most deaf people, I cannot hold an oral conversation with more than two hearing people at once. But with a sign language interpreter, I was able to debate deep issues with a whole room full of hearing people. In essence, sign language was my bridge to the hearing world, not some evil that took me away from it.

Did my message win over all those parents? I don't think so. I still sensed considerable resistance from the strongest opponents. It was actually the hearing parent of a deaf child that had the most impact. Her child had failed in the oral program, and she was very clear in terms of why she was angry and disappointed. Her child had lost valuable time, time that was lost forever. Why didn't anyone recognize this and tell her, back when she could have done something?

Needless to say, this parent had more impact than any of the deaf speakers. Despite all of the information we offered, we were still *different*. Few parents could relate to what deaf people were saying, but they could easily relate to another parent.

If there's a lesson to be learned here, it's something I have already said many times before: Whenever we try to advocate on behalf of Deaf culture, it's inevitable that sometimes we'll feel like we're just banging our heads on the wall. No matter what, every parent wants their child to be *just like them*. Can you blame them? I don't. I'm guilty of doing the same thing. I think my kids should be baseball players and martial artists, just like their daddy. Most likely, I may have to someday deal with the reality that my kids could be computer freaks who hate sports and prefer crossword puzzles to Tae Kwon Do. And I will need to accept it. That's just the way it is.

I understand very well why the world of Deaf culture may seem somewhat intimidating to hearing parents. But it shouldn't be. It improves communication and enriches lives. Like I said, it can bridge worlds together instead of keeping them apart.

To this day I still shake my head in disbelief when I hear the accusation that hearing parents of deaf children will "lose their kids to Deaf culture." It doesn't work that way. The mistake here, in my opinion, is having an either-or mentality (i.e. your child will either sign or he will speak). Reality dictates that if a deaf child can speak, he will. If he can't he won't. Whether or not he signs has virtually no effect on this.

A deaf child who can speak simply adds another language to his repertoire when he signs. This language, ASL, opens more worlds and allows him to enjoy many new experiences which otherwise might not have been accessible. Yet when the situation requires it, this same deaf person can use his oral skills whenever needed. It doesn't have to be either-or. It can be both.

As for the deaf child who can't speak, adding ASL is more than opening new worlds. It's practically a lifesaver. There is nothing more horrific than a deaf child who can neither sign nor speak. This child would encounter language delays, illiteracy, and a frustrating life. But it is frustration that can be remedied with the addition of ASL. So for either scenario, a child who can speak or a child who can't speak, sign language emerges as a definite plus. You can't lose.

Finally, regarding the situation at the Intermediate Unit, the parents agreed to recommend adding sign language to the program. The board subsequently approved the formation of an ad hoc committee to get the ball rolling. Then, in the end, the parents got stonewalled by people at the top who always were and always will be opposed to sign language. Yes, we lost. They still aren't signing over there. Hopefully, there will be more open minds next time around.

ASL: Not Guilty

*T*his has happened so many times I've lost count. A discussion ensues about poor English skills in the deaf community and someone blames ASL. Excessive use of ASL, this person will warn you, causes many a deaf person to lose his grasp of English. What's going on here?

Normally, this would be a topic for the appropriate experts in linguistics to discuss. But I can no longer sit on my hands and watch other people make a scapegoat out of ASL. Therefore I would like to share with you my own deaf perspective on this controversial subject.

Granted, illiteracy in the deaf community is nothing new. It's been a concern for many, many years. I am not surprised at all when people lament the failure of the education system to bring deaf children's reading and writing levels up to par. Yes, we have failed many deaf children. Yes, we must continue striving for newer and better ways to educate them. But no, we do not need to point our fingers at ASL as the source of the problem.

First of all, let's take a moment to remind ourselves about deaf history. Illiteracy, as previously mentioned, is a problem that's been around for a long time. A very long time. Yet if we stop and think about it, ASL has *not* been around for a long time, at least not in classrooms all over the United States. The fact is, for most of the 20th century, sign language was *not* used in the classroom. Oralism was prevalent, sign language was forbidden. Spoken and written English were the primary means of communication. And, as it still is today, illiteracy was a huge problem. And since ASL was not used in the classroom for most of the century, we cannot blame it for the low reading levels all over the country.

On the contrary, after the philosophy of Total Communication was officially adopted around 1976, opportunities for the deaf skyrocketed. Deaf students have had significantly more access to information in the classroom since then and opportunities for advancement (both academically and professionally) have increased dramatically.

Common sense, really. You can't learn anything if you don't understand what your teachers are saying. And it is usually sign language that allows most deaf students to understand what's going on. Look around you and you'll see more deaf administrators, executives, lawyers, businessmen, and entrepreneurs than ever before. Not to sugarcoat anything, mind you. Illiteracy is still a major concern. But if you look carefully at the pattern, ASL has helped more than it has hindered.

In addition to all of this, it is still hard to imagine ASL as the cause of illiteracy because its use in the classroom today is still not as widespread as we might think. For as much as we celebrate ASL, it is actually used by a very small number of teachers.

In the November 1997 issue of *DeafNation*, Trudy Suggs wrote a powerful and sobering article about the number of deaf staff working in deaf schools. The numbers were shockingly low. Only three schools reported that over 40 percent of their staff was deaf. Most schools responded with numbers between 12 and 35 percent. Many schools refused to respond to the survey at all. Another alarming thing to consider is the fact that Suggs was being generous; she included *all* deaf staff in her numbers, including aides, maintenance crews, office assistants, dorm staff, coaches, and so on. Had the survey focused exclusively on teachers and administrators, the results would have been far more disconcerting.

No offense at all is intended to the many hearing teachers of deaf students, who are putting forth an incredible amount of effort and dedication into their jobs. But it's apparent that the number of bona fide, Native ASL-signing staff in deaf schools is very low (I recall one educator, at the 1998 NAD conference, stating that approximately 12 percent of teachers for the deaf are deaf themselves). Therefore, it makes no sense to blame ASL for whatever literacy problems still exist.

Nonetheless, ASL still takes a lot of heat. From time to time I've seen ASL cited as a possible reason for a child's lack of English skills. For example, a testimonial by Otto Menzel, Ph.D., was presented to the United States Senate Subcommittee on Public Health and Safety on February 12th, 1998. Truth be told, he gave a very powerful, accurate report on the state of deaf education. I agreed with him in most aspects until he went off on a tangent that appears to pin the blame on excessive use of ASL for today's disappointing reading levels.

How does ASL wind up taking the blame, anyway? Good question, and I won't pretend to have all the answers. Nonetheless I'd like to take a shot. My guess is that ASL is a victim of guilt by association. Let's take a look, step-by-step, at how ASL often winds up being the bad guy.

Let's say a deaf child is born into a hearing family. Such is the nature of this child's hearing loss that ASL would be the most beneficial means of communication. Unfortunately, his hearing loss is not identified until he's almost two years old. By then, a significant language delay is all but guaranteed.

If, at that stage the parents decide to learn ASL, they still have a formidable barrier to overcome. Not only has their child missed out on two years' worth of language acquisition, but it takes a considerable time (and average of five to seven years, according to information from a Deaf Ed class) for the parents to become fluent in ASL. Considering that the optimal window for picking up language is the first five years of life, we have a real uphill battle in the making.

In most cases, however, hearing parents ultimately prefer or are strongly encouraged to choose the mainstream, oral/audist options. Not to criticize those options, as the kids who *can* thrive in such an environment certainly do. As for the ones who can't, they have lost even more valuable time to acquire language.

Now suppose our hypothetical deaf child has had no language at home and has bounced around from one mainstream program to the other with no success. Eventually, he winds up in a residential school where ASL is encouraged.

Suddenly, with exponentially increased access, he begins to absorb information. He picks up ASL from his peers and from his teachers. His communication and social skills become vastly improved.

Unfortunately, he is still way behind as far as reading and writing skills are concerned. And then comes the erroneous correlation from professionals everywhere: this kid is using ASL but he can't read or write; therefore, it must have been the ASL that caused his poor reading and writing skills.

Meanwhile, whenever a new, innovative teaching strategy involving ASL is proposed, many people in high places hem and haw and are quick to criticize it. The Bi-Bi philosophy, for example, has been scoffed at by many. It has only been around for a relatively short time and is already being blamed for problems that have existed for over a century. It seems to me, quite frankly, that many people are misinformed and perhaps even intimidated by ASL.

Come on. Illiteracy is a serious problem that must be addressed everywhere, not just in the deaf community. If ASL is the cause of poor reading and writing skills, then what about the incredibly high number of *hearing* kids and adults who can't read? It's amazing how many people can speak English fluently yet still can't read or write.

On the other hand, I know many hearing people who are fluent in more than one language; their fluency in a second language does not cause their English to suffer. I feel a need to point this out because I have seen people implying that time spent communicating in ASL takes away from one's ability to use English. That hasn't been my experience. I cite myself, my wife, several relatives, and friends as examples. We code-switch all the time and it doesn't hurt. If anything, I believe it strengthens our minds.

Okay, I've rambled enough. While it's been great defending the merits of ASL, we still have a serious problem with illiteracy, and it's a problem that needs to be addressed everywhere. Perhaps we can tackle this in a future article.

In the meantime... ASL, the verdict is in: not guilty.

The Isolation Myth

*T*he comment was made innocently. No offense was intended and none was taken. But I couldn't help responding to it right away. And, of course, I couldn't resist writing about it later for your reading pleasure. There was a perpetual myth that needed to be dealt with promptly.

A person very interested in Deaf culture recently asked me how deaf people arrive at the decision to "separate themselves into the deaf community or to assimilate themselves into hearing society." Mind you, the individual who asked this question was very much fascinated with the deaf community and she wanted to learn more. Her first lesson, then, was going to be the fact that the deaf community does not "separate" itself from the hearing world.

The truth is that we cannot separate ourselves from hearing society at all. At times I have seen critics of ASL and Deaf culture remark that we "isolate" ourselves from the hearing world, but this is simply not possible. The hearing world is everywhere. We couldn't escape from it even if we wanted to.

Using myself as an example, first let me explain that I'm up to my eyebrows in Deaf culture. I am deaf. My wife Melanie is deaf. My parents are deaf. Melanie's sister Shawna is deaf. Several other relatives are deaf. Melanie and I graduated from Gallaudet University. We are familiar faces at many deaf events, local and national. We both work at the Pennsylvania School for the Deaf, she as a teacher and I as a school counselor. I'm also the secretary for PSD's ASL Committee, yada yada yada. You get the idea. So let's see, with all this beautiful deafness around me, if I can succeed at cutting myself off from the hearing world.

Let's start at my humble abode in Montgomery County, Pennsylvania. Leaving for work early in the morning, I say hello to my hearing neighbor and tell her to have a nice day. Arriving at PSD, I find myself working with plenty of hearing people: hearing teachers, hearing parents, and hearing workers from other agencies. By 11:00 a.m., I've interacted with about thirty hearing people, including the newspaper vendor who shoots the breeze every morning. The number will greatly increase as the day goes by.

My on-the-job interaction with hearing people is modest, I admit, compared to a number of deaf friends who work in other fields. Many of them work for companies where they are the only deaf employees and no one else uses sign language. I consider myself lucky to work in an environment where many people sign.

Around 4:30 the workday is over. Driving home, Melanie and I stop at a restaurant. We order our food from the hearing waiter and pay the hearing cashier when we're done. We go to the mall afterwards and buy a wedding gift for a couple getting married soon. We order and pay for the gift while interacting with a hearing salesperson. Later in the evening I attend my Tai Chi class, where I'm the only deaf student.

At 8:00 p.m., a few phone calls have to be made. Several hearing relatives from my mother's side of the family would like to get together soon. Calling them via TTY, we confirm dinner plans for the following week. Melanie calls her family (all hearing except for her sister) and plans are discussed for an upcoming wedding and a family reunion. I'd like to note that we all have hearing relatives, and they're an important part of our lives no matter whether they sign or not.

By 10:00 p.m. Melanie and I have each had a chance to surf the Internet through our America Online accounts. I spend some time in a deaf newsgroup before moving over to a hearing martial arts group. Incidentally, someone in the deaf newsgroup remarks that ASL isolates deaf children from the world. Unable to keep my mouth shut (so what else is new), I reply with an anecdote that it was my ASL interpreter who prevented me from flunking out of my hearing high school back in the early '80s. As it turned out, ASL did not isolate me from my hearing classmates. More than anything, it bridged the communication gap between us.

All right, that's enough already. You get my drift. It's simply impossible to separate oneself from the hearing world. Hearing relatives, friends, co-workers, classmates, neighbors, waiters and waitresses, the list goes on forever. The world is teeming with hearing people, with no shortage of them in sight. And we will always interact with them in whatever ways we can.

Active involvement in the deaf community does not in any way eliminate a deaf person from the hearing world. There is no either/or, no separation. I really believe that the myths about ASL and Deaf culture isolating deaf children are a result of ignorance, perhaps fear. Sometimes hearing parents may fear that they might lose their child to Deaf culture and that's an understandable concern that can be addressed through proper education.

Sometimes the fear is political. There are certain people who, for whatever reason, oppose ASL. Needless to say, such people may fan the flames of the myth that ASL plus the deaf community equals isolation from the mainstream.

But a person's participation in a core group, in my opinion, is more likely to strengthen rather than to isolate. If I may use my hearing neighbor as an example, she is an avid churchgoer. She faithfully attends Sunday services and participates in many of her congregation's activities. Picnics, bazaars, holiday parties, charity events, church choir, and much more. You name it; she's there. She's a better person for it.

Does this woman's church isolate her from the rest of the world? Not at all. She socializes with people from other denominations and other religions. Our neighborhood is a unique mix of people with different backgrounds and she's friendly with all of us.

Likewise, my core group is the deaf community. It strengthens me and makes me a better person. It gives me a spiritual boost, a sense of belonging. Without it I would feel empty inside. The deaf community adds a spark to my life, a spark I can share with everyone... including the hearing community.

No Deaf Militants

*I*n a recent article, *The Isolation Myth*, I had the pleasure of squashing the stereotype that deaf people are isolated from mainstream society. It was so much fun I thought I'd do it again. This time around, the myth I'd like to smash is the one that says we have deaf militants. So are you ready for some more myth-bashing?

Let's make this clear right now. There are no deaf militants. No such thing. I never saw one, never met one. Never saw a deaf person in army fatigues scaling the walls of a hearing aid facility, covertly breaking in for a search-and-destroy mission. Never saw a deaf person sneak into a cochlear implant factory and reprogram the implants to open garage doors. Never saw a deaf person take deaf children from their hearing parents and raise them as they saw fit. Never saw any kind of activity remotely resembling militant behavior.

All right, maybe there was that little incident in 1988. Something about deaf students shutting down Gallaudet University. But that was warranted. It took some shockingly condescending words and decisions to set off the remarkable chain of events that led to the Deaf President Now protest.

Besides, I still balk at the use of the word "militant" to describe what happened at the DPN protest. The people involved were firm but peaceful; the university was long overdue for a deaf president; and last but not least, DPN had the overwhelming support of local and national politicians, as well as most of the world. It was never an issue of militancy from the deaf. It was an issue of the deaf community initially being ignored and then finally being heard. It was about glass ceilings being shattered, a tremendous step in the right direction. Case closed.

We could end the discussion right here. However, I'd like to add a unique twist to this topic. I'd like to point out the following historical events in my strange life:

- When my hearing loss was identified at age five, hearing doctors and relatives practically pulled the rug out from under my deaf parents. All of us were told not to use sign language.

- Against my will, I was often thrown into a strange booth, fitted with headphones, and asked to decipher sounds and spoken words I couldn't understand.

- Also against my will, I was forced to wear two strange devices on my ears which didn't really help me understand people any better. But boy, did they ever help me hear the toilet go "WHOOOOOOSSSSHHHH!"

- Several times in grade school, an assortment of speech teachers pulled me out of class. With the exception of seeing one real pro who had a great sense of humor, most of this was also against my will.

- A number of times, I had surgery to have tubes put in my ears. I don't recall anyone ever explaining exactly why they were doing this. Regardless of whether these operations were necessary or not, it grew tiresome having so many people constantly poking around in my ears.

- Later I found out that I actually had it easy compared to what my parents went through. They told me stories of teachers whacking them for signing in class. They and many of their classmates were unable to learn this way. Sometimes I wonder why there hasn't been a class-action lawsuit. Lots of deaf people could say, "Hey, if you had allowed me to learn with a language I understood, I could have gone on to... (Fill in the blanks: law school, medical school, etc.)"

As it turns out, countless deaf people have shared similar stories; it's nothing new. It was just shrugged off as the norm for all of us back in those days. That was just the way it was. Deaf people had to accept it and mainstream society thought nothing of it.

Eventually, the deaf community and its supporters spoke up. They began to say, "Hey, you know, ASL is actually a legitimate language. Maybe we should begin using it in schools. Maybe the deaf should be looked at as people with a cultural identity instead of as people with broken ears. Maybe people should value the opinions of deaf adults."

Such audacity! A lot of people in the mainstream didn't like hearing this radical stuff. And thus, the term "deaf militant" was born.

To this day I shake my head in disbelief because no deaf person has ever forced me to do something I didn't want to do. ASL was never forced on me, I was never coerced into joining NAD, and no surgical or psychological procedures were carried out in an effort to make me deafer. Everything I've done in the deaf community has been purely voluntary. So pardon me, I still don't see any deaf militants anywhere.

Okay, enough already. It was fun bashing that myth but it's time to say something positive and constructive for the benefit of any readers I have left. So, did I mention there are no deaf militants? You got it. There are deaf *advocates*. We have plenty of them.

Some are the most charming, diplomatic people you could ever meet. Others are strongly opinionated and don't care if they turn people off. Some of them use tact and sensitivity, respecting your views while politely sharing theirs. Others preach with a "my way or the highway" mentality. Some of them may rub you the wrong way and others may enlighten you. Yes, we have our nice folks and we have our morons, open-minded and narrow-minded people, just like the rest of the world. But militants? I don't think so.

Now if you will excuse me, I have to get going. The Secretary of Deafense is on the phone and we're planning to take Martha's Vineyard back.

Olympic-sized Differences

During the 2000 Olympics in Sydney, Australia, gymnastics was one of the most popular events. World-class athletes performed incredibly difficult routines with remarkable skill and precision, the end result of years and years of training. The whole world, no doubt, was watching in awe. The athletes had elevated themselves to the highest level of competition and in my mind that made them all winners regardless of whether or not they won a medal.

Unfortunately, not everyone feels this way. I almost gagged on my Doritos when the Chinese Olympic Team's coach did an interview on TV. Acknowledging the tremendous pressure to win a gold medal, the coach said something along the lines of "Our country does not recognize a silver or bronze medal. Anything less than gold is simply unacceptable."

After washing down my Doritos with some Coca-Cola, I nearly spewed my drink when a feature on the Romanian team revealed a similar philosophy. They, too, viewed anything other than a gold medal as an abject failure. Inevitably, I realized, a lot of people were going to return to their native homelands in a sour mood. Instead of enjoying the thrill of competition, forming lasting friendships with athletes from other countries, enjoying the sights of Australia, and tons of other enriching experiences, a lot of athletes were going to go home banging their heads on the wall.

I couldn't believe the stuff I was seeing on my 19-inch Sony. Couldn't those gold-crazy foreigners see the error of their ways? More than anything, they needed to sit back and enjoy a nice cold Budweiser. What's wrong with people?

Then, they and other foreign competitors had the chutzpah to criticize our beloved American athletes. Well, eat my Reeboks! They said Americans are too caught up in the commercialization of the Olympics. In short, we're sell-outs.

Hmmm, they might be on to something. In fact, I spilled my Cheerios when a former U.S.A. Olympic track star made a surprise appearance during a news feature. He mentioned he was working for a charitable cause, good for him. Yet at the same time, he repeatedly snuck in a mention of the shoe company that was sponsoring it. Sell-out!

Remember the 1992 Dream Team featuring Michael Jordan? Mike and a few other players almost had to skip the medal ceremony because they had a deal with one shoe company while the Olympics were endorsed by another. Oh, please. Where are the priorities? The athletes or the clothes they wear? They ought to go back to the way the original Olympics were done—with the athletes competing buck-naked. Now *that* would be a ratings boost.

All right, now we have several different perspectives. Perhaps some of the other countries were a bit overzealous about winning. Or, maybe it was just good old-fashioned national pride. There is nothing wrong with the sense of honor that comes from representing your country to the best of your ability.

Perhaps the Americans, marketing endeavors and all, are truly the epitome of success. After all, isn't America the land of opportunity? We're supposed to make a buck; it's the American way. Or, are we shameless sell-outs?

I don't have the answers. But if I may pull the rug out from under this article, (You knew there was a catch, didn't you?) I also don't have the answers for a similar situation regarding the deaf community.

We've seen it for years: people with varying beliefs about deafness, people who don't seem capable of understanding each other. You have one group of people saying that mainstream schools are the way to go, as if it's "the real world" and provides a grade-appropriate academic challenge. Residential schools are just too isolated, they say.

Meanwhile, another group insists that residential schools are the best. Deaf students in residential schools have full access to information, full interaction with their true peers, numerous opportunities to develop leadership skills, and they gain confidence in themselves. Mainstreamed students, they say, miss out on these opportunities and get lost in the crowd—so who's really isolated, then?

Similar arguments arise over sign language versus speech, not to mention the pros and cons of the cochlear implant. I'm not going to get into all of that today; I get a headache just thinking about it.

There are too many people on both sides of the argument, who cannot or will not understand opinions that are different from their own. Like the Olympic athletes who compete for the honor of their country and the ones who compete for a Wheaties endorsement, some people are worlds apart.

Argh, it makes me want to pull my hair out. Yes, the same hair that gets trimmed every month at Ruzzi's for only $14.00 (it's a great deal—this is where you can get the best buzz cut in Pennsylvania). Anyway, apparently we all have a long way to go. Let's find some common ground. In the meantime, have a Coke and smile. I'm going to Disneyworld.

Hear's To You

As a former psychology student, I like to observe and analyze society as it whizzes to and fro, quirks and all. Human nature fascinates me. We're all nuts. I never get tired of it.

Sometimes I like to sit down in a crowded place and watch how hearing people go about their business. I get my kicks watching them fuss over sound-oriented things that ultimately, don't really matter, at least not to a deaf guy like me.

Airports are the best place to people-watch and my favorite part is hanging out at the gate with travelers awaiting their next plane. It is here where I've discovered that hearing people have a device that rivals the cochlear implant: the amazing cellular implant.

A compact device that can be turned on and off at will, this thing is glued to virtually every hearing person's ear. It seems like everyone has one and they can't go anywhere without it. With everyone chittering and chattering into these little cell phones, eyes glazed over as if in a trance, it looks like the Cellular Corporation of the Borg has taken over the country.

The cellular implant—uh, phone—isn't the only sound-based device that has infiltrated hearing culture. On one visit to the airport I saw a group of teenage girls huddled around a strange black box. They were swaying, snapping their fingers, singing and squealing. Who in blue blazes had brainwashed these poor souls?

Taking a closer look, I noticed the girls had slipped a shiny disk into the mysterious black box that pulsated with undecipherable sounds. Sneaking a peek at the disk's container, I saw a picture of three young blond boys. The container said *Hanson*.

Whatever these Hanson boys were saying, it must have been incredibly important. The girls were passionately following every single word. Considering that the average attention span for the typical teenager is about 2.4 seconds, this was indeed a formidable accomplishment.

My curiosity eventually got the best of me and I just had to look up these Hanson kids back home on the Internet. Eagerly anticipating powerful words of wisdom and inspiration, this is what I discovered:

Mmm bop, ba duba dop
Ba du bop, ba duba dop
Ba du bop, ba duba dop
Ba du.

Huh? Say what? Folks, I'm not making this up. Those are the exact lyrics that had the girls squealing in ecstasy. I scratched my head in bewilderment.

The effect that sound has on hearing culture is absolutely incredible. Phones, music, radio, it's everywhere. The effect is mind-boggling and appears to have addictive qualities. I can't help but wonder: *With all this noise bombarding them, do these people ever get a chance to hear themselves think?*

All right, enough already. I've probably alienated all but the most loyal of my hearing friends. It's time to get right to the point. That is: for its own sanity, the deaf community needs to understand how important sound is to the average hearing person.

Why, you ask? So we can modify our approach, put ourselves in the hearing guy's shoes, and come up with creative ways to educate hearing people that we can do just fine without the frequent input of sound. And, if we fail to enlighten the hearing folks, at least we can understand why they feel the way that they do.

The fact is, sound is what connects everyone in the hearing world. It is the most popular medium that hearing people use to exchange information. It is the basis of communication, education, and entertainment. For most hearing people, the idea of life without sound is simply incomprehensible. The mere thought of losing their hearing freaks them out.

So if you say you're proud to be deaf, more power to you—but be prepared to get a lot of weird looks. Be prepared to tactfully explain how you can thrive in the visual world of sign language, gestures, facial expressions, TTYs, books, newspapers, and computers. For good measure, explain that you can utilize your other senses more than adequately enough to compensate for your lack of hearing. But brace yourself for the frustration that comes when people don't seem to get it.

Don't let it get to you. Cherish the hearing people who do get it, and be patient with those who don't.

Maintain a healthy sense of humor, understand how different your world of deafness is, and celebrate that difference. Above all, be glad that you're not among the millions who can't shake that annoying *Mmmbop ba duba dop* out of their heads. *Ba du bop, ba duba dop...*

Men Are Pigs

*M*en are pigs. Yes, me too. I leave the toilet lid up. I spit. I scratch. I don't deny it. I never cared much about it until now. Most of this article is for couch potato Neanderthals like me. Something came up that has me a bit concerned about my chest-thumping brethren.

What happened was I got an e-mail from a deaf woman asking me how she could get her hearing husband and kids interested in learning ASL. From the tone of her e-mail, she appeared to be rather frustrated.

Answering on behalf of the kids was easy enough. I surmised that if ASL was presented in a fun and interesting way, most kids would find it enjoyable. I recommended an ASL CD-ROM program featuring plenty of fun ASL lessons and games.

As for the husband, I hedged a bit. Sure, I figured, if a deaf woman told her hearing boyfriend or husband how important ASL was to her, then that boyfriend or husband would certainly put in the time and effort to learn. However, a grim reality lurked in the back of my mind.

Face it, it's the truth: a high percentage of hearing men simply do not bother learning sign language. It's personally starting to annoy me. Up until now I've been loyal to my fellow male pigs, vociferously defending our right to burp, scratch, and watch Monday Night Football, but not any longer.

Why am I annoyed with hearing members of my own gender, you ask? It's simple. Every time a deaf guy I know dates or marries a hearing woman, 90 percent of the time that woman signs. Even if the guy has exceptional speech and residual hearing, the woman still goes out of her way to learn sign language. But when a deaf girl finds a hearing boyfriend, sheeesh, it's a totally different story.

Anytime my wife and I visit one of my friends, my wife is guaranteed a good time because my friends have wives and girlfriends who sign fluently. But when my wife and I visit her friends, I'm often uncomfortable because their husbands/boyfriends don't sign worth peanuts. Conversation rarely goes beyond the superficial "How ya doing" and "Nice car." Basically, my wife gets to chat up a storm with my friends' significant others while I'm stuck twiddling my thumbs with hers.

The same thing often applies to hearing families of deaf people. Hearing mothers and sisters appear to know and use more sign language than most fathers and brothers. Aunts and nieces also seem to have the upper hand over uncles and nephews. No, this is not scientifically proven; this is all subjective, and I know there are exceptions. But I've personally seen enough to surmise that the females are running circles around the males in the sign language department.

So why the discrepancy? After asking around, a

couple of theories popped up. Theory one: Men are pigs, just because hey, we're *men.* Most men, especially macho types, are not too crazy about self-disclosure, sharing feelings, and communicating (barf!). The very nature of ASL requires that you reveal your thoughts and feelings through visual expression. You simply cannot use ASL with a poker face. Through ASL, you often allow others to see your innermost feelings.

Yuck! I can just see the Chicago Bears' Fan Club running for the exits, trying their best not to puke. For most deaf men, this is not an issue because they've been signing all their lives. But when it comes to hearing guys, I can see how they might not be too turned on by the expressive, aesthetic nature of ASL.

Theory number two came from a good friend who happens to be a sign language instructor. By her own admission, she feels that in some sign language classes, there is a subtle amount of male-bashing. Classes are usually full of women who are happy just to get away from their lazy, dirty-socks-on-the-floor husbands. So when one innocent male soul signs up for ASL 101, the ladies let him have it.

I haven't seen this phenomenon myself. Quite the opposite, I know of some guys who have signed up for ASL solely because they knew the classes were packed with women. Nonetheless, my ASL instructor friend insists that slowly, subtly, some women pick and peck at the men until they wind up with no motivation to return to class.

Even if the female students are being nice, it's still hard on the guys because conversation amongst classmates most likely focuses on women's issues. That's understandable. I can only join my wife's conversations with her friends to a certain point before I chuck it and reach for the sports pages. Hey, we're *men*.

Some people may challenge my assessment of the knuckle-dragging, oops, I mean male species. My response to them is: go ahead, walk into any sign language class and observe the disproportionate ratio of women to men (if there any men in there at all).

Rather than male-bashing, however fun that may be, I would just like this article to serve as a wake-up call. My observations are, as I admitted, entirely subjective and based wholly upon my own personal experiences. For all I know, there could be a large number of ASL-competent men out there whom I've never had a chance to meet.

But if you know a hearing guy who has ties to the deaf community and he doesn't sign, do me a favor: get him to drop the remote and drag him to the nearest ASL class. Thank you!

We're Fine, Thank You

*U*h-oh. For the fourth time in ten years, I was exposed to the chicken pox virus. A colleague at work came down with it and she would be out for two weeks. On top of that, my grandmother came down with shingles—a different form of the disease, but essentially the same virus and equally contagious.

I scratched my head and wondered if I'd be doing a lot more scratching in a couple of weeks. The reason for my concern: I have never had the chicken pox. No one in my family recalls me ever having caught it, and there are no medical records documenting any such incidence of the itchy illness.

Either I have an uncanny natural immunity, or somebody missed something when I was a kid. Deciding to find out for myself, once and for all, I asked my mother to dig up my old pediatric records. My pediatrician had long since passed away, but he had sent us my file many years ago after I switched to our current family doctor. The file was old, yellowing, and full of scribbled notes, relics from an era preceding fancy computers and word processors.

Alas, I could find no mention of chicken pox. But I did find some rather interesting, eye-opening stuff. Among the usual immunization records and medical history were some letters and other correspondence from a number of otolaryngologists who operated on me in the past, putting tubes in my ears on numerous occasions.

Actually, the technical mumbo-jumbo did not interest me. Instead, it was one particular comment that jumped out and grabbed my attention. It was in a letter dated March 4, 1975. Here's what it said:

This is an unfortunate lad with two mute parents.

Can you believe this? All right, we shouldn't be too harsh. That was just the way people perceived deafness back then. They didn't mean any harm; times change, you know. However, there's a message in there somewhere if we compare the different eras of then and now.

Back then, the perception of deafness was, if I may respectfully quote the doctor, *unfortunate*. It was a pathological condition, nothing more. No formal recognition of ASL as a language, no signing permitted in deaf schools, no Deaf President Now, no TTYs, no captioned TV, no Internet, no nothing.

So maybe my doctor wasn't too far off base— perhaps, relatively speaking, deafness was indeed somewhat *unfortunate*, from a doctor's perspective, of course (I can just see my folks saying, "Hey, waitaminute, those were the good old days!").

All right, that was then and this is now. In today's present time, my poor (ahem) *mute* parents are not doing too bad. They both have comfortable jobs. Their salaries, not that it's anyone's business, allow them a comfortable living. While they're not going to own a remote island somewhere in the Caribbean, they will be in relatively good shape when they retire.

And how about yours truly, this *unfortunate lad?* I'm doing fine, thank you. I enjoy working as a counselor and as a writer. I consider myself very fortunate and I thank my family for their love and support.

This is not intended to be a told-you-so open letter to the doctors who implied that my family and I would lead difficult, unfortunate lives. Rather, I think we should all take note at how attitudes, increased sensitivity, and accessibility have helped us all to come a long way.

The most obvious difference, I believe, is the boom in technology and deaf rights. It's so easy to take this stuff for granted. Just today, for example, I sent e-mail to several friends. Some of these friends actually live in other countries. Back in the early '70s, however, it was hard enough communicating with people who lived just down the street.

Before TTYs became prevalent, the only means of catching up on the news was at weekly or monthly gatherings, many of them at the local deaf club. I also remember how many of my parents' friends would drop by for a visit unannounced because there was no convenient way to set a date or time. This problem was alleviated when the TTY was brought into our lives, and at the time it was a real godsend. But it was still a huge, enormous machine that looked like a mailbox on steroids. The keys were spaced wide apart and the whole contraption dwarfed me when I used it as a kid.

Nowadays, of course, we have e-mail, pagers, and state-of-the-art TTYs. Today's TTYs, which are portable, lightweight and with many convenient features, make a phone conversation much more enjoyable (never mind that in a few years, phone conversation will be practically obsolete).

While there are several other technical advances we could discuss (captioned TV, relay services, etc.), I think one of the biggest improvements of today's era is accessibility in the workplace. Way back when, job opportunities for the deaf were significantly less than they are now. There are several factors responsible for this.

Number one, I strongly believe that when sign language was finally permitted in the classroom, this allowed many deaf people to learn faster through the language they knew best. It's a simple concept: the more you understand, the more you learn.

Number two, the Americans with Disabilities Act (ADA) has opened many doors. Accessibility has improved exponentially since the '60s and '70s, and more deaf people are furthering their education. In addition to well-known programs such as those at Gallaudet, NTID, and CSUN, many deaf people have the option of attending hearing universities with interpreters and notetakers provided. More deaf people are becoming doctors, lawyers, engineers, entrepreneurs, and so on.

Speaking of doctors, I wish to repeat that my doctors meant no offense. In their correspondence, where they often mentioned my *unfortunate* deaf family, they genuinely felt bad. They genuinely felt that it was going to be one heck of a cold, cruel world out there, and that there was not much they could do to fix it.

And *fix it*... that's a job doctors are paid to do, one they do quite well. They fixed my hernia. They fixed that problem I had with my (since removed) tonsils. They fixed my broken thumb and skillfully handled other maladies that came my way. But they could not do much to fix my ears, and thus I was *unfortunate*.

Times do change, however, and people are starting to understand that deafness does not always have to be *unfortunate*. My wife and I recently took our son, Darren, to his pediatrician for a checkup. This pediatrician happens to know sign language, which is one of the reasons we chose him. On this particular day he was not in, so another doctor came in to look at Darren. This doctor gave Darren a clean bill of health and then suddenly she became very concerned. She glanced at me and then at my wife.

"Since you're both deaf," she began, "I'm wondering if Darren might be deaf. I'm concerned because..." she suddenly stopped herself in mid-sentence. To my surprise, she smacked herself on the head.

"Oh, never mind, you both know sign language!" She just realized that even if Darren had a hearing loss, he would still have access to language in our household. It's so nice to see a person who gets it.

Now that I've sufficiently proven that life doesn't have to be *unfortunate*, it's time for me to turn my efforts elsewhere. Namely, volunteering my time at medical clinics. Specialists could do experiments to figure out what makes me particularly immune to chicken pox. If they can get to the bottom of this, they could...

Huh? They already have a chicken pox vaccine? Aw, man. There goes my Nobel Prize.

Don't Feed the Deafies

*T*he kid was staring at us. Not with the innocent, childlike curiosity I'm used to, but with a probing look that said *what the hell is wrong with them?* As my wife and I signed to each other in a restaurant, we had this kid's undivided attention.

Normally, I respond to kids with a smile, a wink, or some kind of thumbs-up. But this kid was different. About ten years of age, he kept his eyes glued on us, non-stop. His mother gave him a sharp reprimand: *Junior, don't stare at the nice deaf people!* It was like zookeepers saying don't feed the deafies, uh, bears.

But Junior was persistent. Not only did he keep staring, but soon he turned to his younger sister and made fun of our signing.

At that moment the temptation was too great. I noticed the kid was talking with his mouth full and I wanted to respond in kind with my own display of seafood. (Seafood, see food, get it?) I wanted to take a huge bite out of my hamburger then open my mouth and go, "Blaaahhh! This is what *you* look like! So there!"

67

Chivalrous gentleman that I am, I asked my wife for permission to unleash my Inner Neanderthal. Of course, she kicked me in the shin and said no. Unless I wanted to sleep in the garage, I had to behave myself.

A few days later, my wife and I were in line at the supermarket, waiting to check out our groceries. Again, we were signing in public, and again, we elicited an unusual response.

This time around there was a middle-aged couple in front of us. The woman was talking up a storm. The man was nodding half-heartedly, a classic case of "Yes, dear, no, dear, whatever you say, dear." I truly felt sorry for him.

And then he noticed us. The way our signing caught him off guard, it was obvious he had never seen a deaf person before. He had a puzzled look on his face, which was understandable.

His wife, however, didn't miss a beat. Without even pausing to take a breath, she immediately switched the subject and began talking about deafness.

"Oh, they're deaf people," she began. I could read her lips somewhat and could see that she was giving her husband an impromptu lesson in Deafness 101.

"Because they can't hear, they communicate with their hands," she continued. It took every ounce of willpower to resist scratching my head and going, *"Duh, really?"*

Our talkative friend was nowhere near finished. "Some deaf people wear hearing aids but others choose not to," she went on. "They also have special schools where the teachers use sign language."

This lady was amazing. Some jokester must have had her in mind when the following prank advertisement was circulated:

Encyclopedia Britannica for Sale. Mint Condition, Never Used. Freaking Wife Knows Everything.

But as brilliant as she was, she forgot that deaf people also read lips—which her husband figured out when he realized I was watching the conversation. He had a pained look on his face and smiled apologetically as his wife kept rambling. I think she managed to cover every detail of the deaf community, including our mating habits.

Most of the time, I admire it when a hearing person shows such thorough understanding of deafness. Deaf awareness is very important to me and if I had to grade this woman on her expertise, she certainly earned an "A." But what bugged me was the way she approached the subject. Without even acknowledging we were there, without even saying a polite hello, she just kept talking about us as if she were tour guide at the local zoo's primate exhibit.

Again, temptation beckoned. I wanted to tap the lady on the shoulder and ask for a banana. I wanted to thump my chest and say, "Me Deffman, you Jane. Deffman like banana. Ooga!" If she was going to talk about me like I was an orangutan, it's the least I could do to oblige.

But once more, the threat of having to sleep in the garage won out. I smiled at the husband and he gave an appreciative nod. Other than the fact that we were both seriously whipped, we also shared something else in common: dignity.

As gratifying as it would have been to make a scene, I knew it would have been wrong. Yes, my wife was right after all. As prudish as it may seem, we all have a responsibility to maintain our composure and resist the oh-so-tempting snappy comebacks.

Look at it this way: society is all too eager to slap a label or stereotype on any group of people. Although we'd like to believe that we live in an enlightened era of tolerance and understanding, discrimination and pre-conceived notions remain rampant.

I recall how many deaf children, simply because they could not understand their teachers (or professional evaluators such as doctors, psychologists, speech therapists, etc), were unfairly documented as being "rude", "inattentive", "highly distractible", and so on. This type of misunderstanding and overgeneralization continues to this very day, in more ways than one.

So, if you're the first deaf person a hearing guy has ever met, make me proud. Hold your head up high and rise above it if for whatever reason people react strangely around you (remember the problem is them, not you). If someone gives you a funny look, then just look him in the eye, smile, and walk on. You'll be glad you did.

All right, enough of that already. Me want banana.

Academic Freedom

*Q*uick, think back to your high school days. What are the first things that come to mind? If you're like most people, you probably thought of dear friends, exciting events, or perhaps a favorite teacher who always made you laugh.

But what about academics? Do you remember the quadratic formula? How about Newton's laws of motion? Would you be able to explain them in perfect detail if someone asked you? If you studied a foreign language, do you actually use it every now and then (and fluently at that)? If you are like me, the answer to all of the above is nope, nada, zilch, and zippo.

So what's the purpose of school, then? It does appear that there is some degree of truth to the book that boldly declares, *Everything I Need to Know, I Learned in Kindergarten.*

Granted, grade school and high school provide the building blocks for skills you use throughout your life. But the odds are, most people latch onto one primary skill and continue to develop it further beyond their academic years.

71

For example, if you loved computer science in high school, then that's what stuck with you if later on you became a computer programmer or website designer. But as for the other courses—foreign languages, history, social studies, home economics, English literature, and much more—who remembers? I don't.

Creative writing was my one true joy in high school. All of the advice my teachers offered sticks with me to this very day. But what about math? Nope. History? I can't even remember what I did yesterday, let alone what some Mongolian invaders did in the year, uh, whatever.

So if I can't remember any history or math, what's the point? Why did we even bother? If I can't recall a danged thing from Mrs. Kerr's history class or Mrs. Wagner's geometry class, then did we waste each other's time?

Absolutely not. Mrs. Kerr, Mrs. Wagner, and several other inspiring teachers gave me something far more valuable than the stuff you find in textbooks: they gave me academic freedom.

Granted, I hardly remember anything they taught. But I do remember the *way* they taught, and it changed my whole line of thinking. These teachers often asked: "What do *you* think?" They bombarded their students with 'what if' questions as much as possible.

It was Mrs. Kerr who woke me up by critiquing a paper for being too factually accurate. I had simply regurgitated factual information from a textbook and she wasn't satisfied.

"Come on, Mark," she implored. "Put yourself in the Emperor's shoes. Imagine yourself being right there. What are you thinking? How does it feel? What do you want? What errors in judgment might you make in the heat of the moment? What if you did things a bit differently?"

My brain was spinning. She dared me to be original, to challenge conventional wisdom, to look behind the scenes. We got rid of "the box" long before they invented the catch-phrase, "think outside the box."

What's the big deal, you ask? It's a big deal to me because I don't think we've done enough of this for deaf students. We need to continually encourage our deaf youth to think for themselves.

The most important question you can ask deaf students—actually, *any* student—is still "What do you think?" This is essential because it shows students their opinion is valued and that they can indeed have an impact in this world.

For example, recently I witnessed a nice class presentation where the kids were in charge. They needed to summarize everything they'd learned that year, and they had to present it in such a way that it would be appealing to incoming students and their parents. The goal was made clear, but how they got there was entirely up to them.

They did just fine. They delegated their own assignments and chose various presentation methods (bulletin boards, posters, PowerPoint, and an assortment of graphs, charts, and color photography). Their overall presentation was a success. But as much as I enjoyed the end result, I also enjoyed the process leading up to it.

Ten years from now, they may or may not remember the factual details of their presentation. But they will definitely remember the exhilarating freedom that came with planning their own project.

They will incorporate the leadership skills that emerged from this experience.

Unfortunately, not all deaf students are blessed with such open-minded staff. Many have to tolerate a *sit down and shut up* mentality. In essence, they are simply put in their place. Their creativity is suppressed, not allowed to shine through at all.

In Lou Ann Walker's fascinating book, *A Loss for Words*, she shares an experience where a deaf student in an auto body shop completely loses his cool. His teacher simply asked him a "what if" question, wanting to know what the student thought about an alternative method for assembling an engine. It was a method that was not in the textbook, but just as effective nonetheless.

The student, who was used to being told exactly what to do, couldn't handle the opportunity to think for himself. Too many years of *sit down and shut up* had turned him into an automaton. It was the first time he had a teacher open-minded enough to challenge his thinking, but it came too late. He snapped and threw one of his tools at the teacher. Do we want this for the next generation of deaf students? I don't.

We need to ensure that deaf students have a safe yet challenging academic environment where questions, not automotive parts, are tossed around freely. Not only should we ask students more questions; we should encourage them to question us. Look at it this way: are we telling them what to think, or are we teaching them how to think? It's a big difference. Think about it.

The Other Half of Bi-Bi

*S*teven (name changed for privacy) was once again sitting in my office. I hadn't seen him in three years and his visit was a pleasant surprise. Having been out of touch for so long, I was curious to find out what he'd been up to. Years ago, I predicted this kid would be the next Albert Einstein. This is the kid who, at age 12, often discussed the theory of relativity and the possibility of time travel. When he graduated I told him to keep up the good work and let me know when he invented the first space shuttle with warp drive capacity.

Three years later, I thought he came back to show off his recent Nobel Peace Prize. I was wrong. The brainy kid was now an exasperated teenager. Rather than celebrating academic success, he lamented how he got a bum deal in life. He has a major concern that he thinks all deaf people should be made aware of.

Yes, Steven may be able to explain how traveling at the speed of light could hypothetically slow down an astronaut's aging process. But in spite of his sharp mind, he has one glaring weakness: he can't put his tremendous knowledge on paper. As he puts it in no uncertain terms:

"My English is lousy."

"But Steven," I protested. "You might have a weakness in one area, but you can work on it. You still have so many strengths. You can still become a great scientist."

"Nope," said Steven. "I can't be a scientist if my English is lousy. I can't prove anything on paper. I can't write a good hypothesis. I can't write up a detailed experiment. I can't write a convincing conclusion. I'm pissed off."

Steven was stuck. There wasn't much more I could say or do, except ask if remedial English courses could help him catch up.

"I don't know," he replied. "I wish they taught me this a long time ago." Steven hit the nail on the head. He's right, you know. This happens to be a widespread, serious problem.

Don't get me wrong; I still believe that ASL is the key to learning. In my opinion, ASL in the classroom empowers thousands of deaf students, allowing many of them to process information far more efficiently than any other method. From personal experience, I can vouch for this. I floundered in high school until I got an ASL interpreter. In college, I thrived at Gallaudet because everyone was signing. ASL is access to information, so signing is not really the issue here.

However, we must remember that ASL is only half of the Bi-Bi equation. The other half, of course, is English. When we talk about bilingual and bicultural, we have ASL and Deaf culture on one side, English and hearing culture on the other. To succeed in this world we need to build a bridge between both sides. Our ability to cross this bridge, quite frankly, depends on our ability to master English. For as much as we rightfully demand that hearing people understand the benefits of ASL, we too need to understand the benefits of English.

ASL is power because it gives deaf people access to information. With it, we learn more. English is also power. It is another avenue to information in the form of books, newspapers, and computers. It's also a bridge to the hearing world and major job markets, like it or not. It doesn't really matter if you can sign or speak fluently; if you don't have adequate reading and writing skills, your options are limited. That's a fact of life that we can't ignore.

Some people in the deaf community have strongly disagreed with me on this issue. "ASL is our language," they say. "We don't need English." Uh-huh. While I understand and share pride in ASL, I still think it's professional suicide to ignore English. There are plenty of jobs out there, entry level and higher, where your boss will ask you to take a test to measure your written English skills. It's obvious that without English, it's hard to move up the corporate ladder.

Here we go, opening up an old can of worms: standardized tests. Ick. Tell me you don't think they're fair, and I'll agree with you wholeheartedly. I've bombed on many of them myself. But that's the way the ballgame is played, fair or not. It's unfortunate. I know of several deaf people who are excellent teachers yet they don't have a steady teaching job because they can't pass their state's certification exam. Many of these teachers, while under temporary/emergency certification, have had a significant impact on deaf students they've worked with. Often, they were the only staff that signed native ASL in their respective schools. Not surprisingly, many students responded positively and were able to learn at a faster pace.

Yet when the time came for these teachers to obtain official state certification, they failed the tests and were soon on their way out. Probably not fair. There's definitely a cultural bias screwing a lot of qualified people out of jobs—not just the deaf, but other minorities as well. Unfortunately, complaining about it doesn't work. So what can we do?

Right now, the only solution I can think of is to master the other half of the Bi-Bi equation. If we master both ASL and English, we have more power. There would be more deaf professionals, deaf professionals with societal and political clout. I would really like to see more deaf professionals out there because we are seriously under-represented in lots of high places. And, to get into those high places, we need to master the language that the people there are using: English.

That's enough of that. This article is for Steven. He's not giving up. He's going back to school. He's going to try to master the other half of Bi-Bi. He's strongly encouraging other deaf students to follow his example. Whether or not he eventually invents warp drive, he's already blazing a path for the next generation.

Raising the Bar

In the middle of my presentation on *Everything You Wanted to Know About Deafness but Were Afraid to Ask,* a hand shot up. It was an eighth grade student from Germantown Friends School, which is right across the street from the Pennsylvania School for the Deaf. GFS students have been learning sign language and doing volunteer work at PSD for the past few years; as a former GFS student myself, it's a great thrill to see the hearing world of my past meshing beautifully with the deaf world I live in today.

But this kid, this eighth-grader, had a question that floored me. I had just explained how I lost my hearing at age five and struggled through hearing schools until age fourteen, when I finally got a sign language interpreter in the ninth grade. It was this access to language, the use of ASL, which allowed me to process information at a much faster rate.

"But if you lost your hearing at age five," the boy asked, "how did you continue to learn English? Shouldn't you have been stuck at the

79

reading level of a five-year-old? How did you keep learning through grade school?"

What a question! I was used to answering queries such as "Can deaf people drive?" and "How do you use the phone?" This one had me absolutely stumped.

Hmm, let's see. I know. I'm a deaf child of deaf parents, a DOD. Therefore I always had access to language no matter what. Yeah, true, to some extent. But then again, my parents were strongly discouraged from signing with me back then, what with the prevalent oral philosophy of those days.

Okay, then. Perhaps it was speaking with my hearing friends and relatives that allowed me to further develop my English skills. Whoops, waitaminute, that can't be it. I was deaf as a post, so how could I consistently learn new words if I was always struggling to understand what people were saying?

There is only one possible answer left: reading. Yup, that's it. Books, newspapers, comic books, magazines, you name it. As I got older, closed-captioned TV was also thrown into the mix. Yes, that must be it. No matter whether I was hearing, hard of hearing or deaf, there was always one constant: reading. Lots and lots of reading. Now that I think about it, my parents and grandparents read children's books to me all the time when I was a toddler. My love for the written word grew each day. Soon I was off and reading on my own, anything I could get my hands on.

I especially loved reading *Encyclopedia Brown* during my early grade school years and soon moved on to the *Alfred Hitchcock and the Three Investigators* mystery series by the fourth grade. I had an immense love for the popular *Archie* comics and then graduated (much to my mother's dismay) to the crude but funny *MAD Magazine*.

But the biggest influence of them all was Bill Conlin, an award-winning sports columnist for the *Philadelphia Daily News*. I'm going to use him as an example to drive home the key point of this article: the importance of raising the bar.

Before we can talk about Conlin, it needs to be pointed out that on several occasions people have offered me some friendly advice regarding my own writing style.

"Hey, that's great stuff you wrote," someone would say. "But you've got to go easy on the vocabulary. It's too hard for most deaf people. You've got to use more simple words."

I don't think so. I will not dumb down, and do not intend to.

This is where Bill Conlin comes in. Let me tell you, I'm a certifiable baseball nut, a rabid fan of the Philadelphia Phillies; I've been following them for as long as I can remember. One of the best parts of being a Phillies fan is reading about them in the *Daily News*. The *Daily News*, pardon my bias, is the best sports paper in the country. Conlin's articles were, and still are, my favorite.

Conlin is no ordinary journalist. He's the master of metaphor, the most unbelievably creative writer I've ever seen. Were he not a sports freak himself, he would probably be writing screenplays and winning awards at the Cannes Film Festival. Yes, he's that good. You'd never expect to see such imaginative prose in a sports column but this guy is one of a kind.

Way back when I was a snot-nosed nine-year-old, you might have thought that Conlin's use of metaphors, idioms, dry humor, and innuendo would fly over my head. Sometimes, it did. But such was my love for the Phillies that I would read on and *absorb*. I would be so caught up in an article that if I didn't know the meaning of a word, I would ask someone or look it up. And, in many cases, that wouldn't be necessary. It was easy to figure out what a word meant solely by the context in which it was used.

For example, if a pitcher was *inconsolable* after losing an important game, crying in his beer while teammates tried to cheer him up, it's easy to guess what *inconsolable* means even if you've never seen the word before.

The bottom line, pure and simple, is the fact that continued and consistent exposure to new words promotes learning. When we allow ourselves to be handcuffed by that damned statistic, the one that reminds us how most deaf people read at the third or fourth grade level, we have this tendency to lower our standards. Don't fall into this trap! Raise the bar, and keep pushing it higher.

At PSD, it's pleasing to see how the staff is keeping this in mind. I was thrilled when Principal Marsha Miceli recently spoke to PSD parents about the magnitude of language acquisition. She credits former MKSD superintendent Gertie Galloway for a very important point she still shares with parents and staff:

Using the word "earthquake" as an example, she demonstrated how new words are learned. Supposing there was an actual earthquake somewhere, a hearing child would hear the word "earthquake" on TV, on the radio, in parents' conversation, in other people's conversation, and again in the classroom. By the time he heard it in the classroom, this hearing child would have been exposed to the word "earthquake" so much that he would have already assimilated it into his vocabulary. (If I remember correctly, a child needs to hear or see a word approximately 30 to 35 times before it becomes an integral part of his own vocabulary bank.)

Most deaf children, unfortunately, miss out on this opportunity. They will not hear it on the radio, in neighbors' everyday conversation, or anywhere else. And, if their parents cannot communicate effectively with them, they are totally out of the loop. So, when they finally see the word "earthquake" in the classroom, they might have no clue what it means. The next time they're exposed to the word "earthquake" may have to be the next time there is an actual earthquake. Simply put, it takes plenty of earthquakes, uh, exposure, before new words can truly have meaning for them.

If we insist on dumbing down, if we insist on keeping our vocabulary simple because it's supposedly too hard for most deaf people, then we allow the problem to continue. If there's no medium where kids can be consistently exposed to new words, their vocabulary won't grow. Which is precisely why we need to encourage a love for reading. Children's books, comic books, newspapers, sports columns, gossip columns, I don't care what it is. As long as reading is enjoyable, as long as new words are introduced, it's all for the good. Keep raising the bar. Before you know it, kids all over the country will understand why the Phillies are the most exciting team in the National League.

Editor's note: PSD principal Marsha Miceli contributed to this article.

Men Are Pigs II

*L*ong time ago in a galaxy far, far, away—all right, when I was writing for another newspaper—I once wrote an article titled "Men Are Pigs." It was a great opportunity to vent my frustration at hearing pi... uh, men.

As I explained it, there's a very noticeable pattern when deaf people date or marry hearing people. When a deaf man is with a hearing woman, most of the time that hearing woman is sensitive enough to learn sign language. After all, women truly understand the value of effective communication.

Men, on the other hand, think effective communication means not burping during player introductions at the Super Bowl. So, when a hearing man dates a deaf woman, a great majority of the time that man does not learn sign language. Of course, there are some wonderful guys who are exceptions, but they are few and far between.

For the most part, whenever my wife and I visit her deaf friends who have hearing husbands or boyfriends, I'm often left in the dark. It's not unusual for me to wind up in the company of a guy who can only gesture, "Want another beer?"

Recently, however, I truly felt sympathy for the non-signing guy. While my wife and I were visiting this couple—actually, it was a hearing-hearing couple, not deaf-hearing—the woman signed and of course the guy did not. But since his wife was hearing and he himself had no ties to the deaf community, I could understand. Is he supposed to learn ASL because his wife has one friend who happens to be deaf? Sure, it would be nice, but let's be realistic. We're talking about men here.

So, as this guy squirmed in discomfort, I did my best to make polite conversation. Nothing deep, just some superficial how-do-ya-do's. And then it happened: my wife and her friend just got up and left the room. The two of them had been a bridge between their communicatively incompetent hubbies, so there was a sense of safety in numbers. Not anymore.

There we were, two idiots sitting there, incapable of holding a decent conversation. The silence was deafening, no pun intended. At that moment, a tempting thought hit me: wouldn't it be great if, for once, we guys could say what was really on our minds?

"So, Bill... I'm deaf as a post and can't understand a word you're saying. Doesn't that suck?"

"Yeah, and I can't sign worth peanuts. Isn't this stupid?"

"Darn right. What the hell were our wives thinking, leaving us hanging like this?"

"Yeah! How come they always go to the bathroom together? Do they need some kind of help? I know four-year-olds who can go to the potty themselves. What's the deal with this? "

"Ah, a woman's bathroom is different. It's like a bar lounge. They're in there drinking pina coladas and watching us on closed-circuit television. They're probably laughing at how pathetic we are."

"They can kiss my hearing butt." (High five) "Want another brewski?"

Unfortunately, this conversation never happened. Instead, we sweated through ten eternities—okay, okay, ten minutes—of awkward silence before we found an even better solution: FOOTBALL!

That's right. We turned on the TV and watched a great game. We didn't have to say another word to each other for the rest of the night. It was beautiful.

And so, we come to the moral of the story: Men are still pigs. But come on, we can work through this. Ladies, please drag your man to the nearest sign language class. He'll thank you later. Men—both deaf and hearing—hang tight, and be patient. Try to meet each other halfway. And, if all else fails, you still have the NFL.

Super Phony

*T*he phone suddenly rang in my office, snapping me out of a paperwork-induced fog. It was 2:30 p.m. on an otherwise uneventful Monday afternoon. The administrative secretary was on the line with an unexpected surprise. I jumped out of my seat when she told me that Cindy, a former high school classmate, was in the headmaster's office. I hadn't seen her in fifteen years.

Cindy was in town for the class of 1984's fifteenth reunion, which I had skipped. She was staying in Philadelphia for an extra day and thought she'd surprise me at work.

I rushed over to the administration building with much excitement and anticipation. This was a dear friend, one of a handful of students in my class who had put in the effort to learn sign language. I was the only deaf student in the whole school and really appreciated her being sensitive to my communication needs.

As a matter of fact—I won't deny this—there was a time when I thought Cindy was absolute hot stuff. Tall, sexy, good-looking, intelligent, a great sense of humor, the total package. I had a bit of a crush on her in high school but never really did anything about it. After all, she was one of few people who could really communicate with me. I valued her friendship far too much to risk letting my raging teenage hormones ruin everything. The fact remains, though: This girl was hot, hot, hot!

And there we were, reunited once more, fifteen years later. I was in awe as we greeted each other in the headmaster's office. She was still an attractive and dynamic woman. In fact, more so than ever before, she was no longer a perky high school student; she was now a sexy, demure, full-grown professional. On top of that, she was now *Doctor* Cindy, having earned her Ph.D. in veterinary medicine. Oh boy, all this and brains, too! And she also...

Whack!

Ouch. That was my wife Melanie, bashing me on the head with a roller pin. Quit slobbering and get to the point already, she says. Okay, okay, I'm getting there. The point is, it was awesome seeing Cindy again. I was thrilled to catch up on the news with this very interesting and fascinating person. But something was different. In fact, in my mind, I asked myself one question:

What the hell was I thinking?

As impressed as I was with who Cindy had become, as happy as I was to see her, I realized we were as romantically compatible as oil and water. It had always been that way. Don't get me wrong; it's irrelevant anyway. I've been happily married to Melanie since 1994 and there is no one else remotely close in the way she is able to relate to me. Nonetheless, the question still perturbed me:

What the hell was I thinking?

I was completely taken aback at how my perspective had changed since those good old high school days. In 1984, I worshipped the ground Cindy walked on. Hey, she could sign a bit, she could *communicate*. Compared to the four hundred or so other girls who couldn't sign at all, Cindy was a goddess.

Fifteen years later, Cindy still has some signing skills, for which I'm grateful. Nonetheless, things have changed significantly ever since I've become a member of the deaf community. Today, I'm very comfortable in the presence of others who sign ASL fluently. Especially my wife, Melanie, roller pin and all.

That's what struck me so hard. In 1984, when few people in my world signed, Cindy was *the bomb*. She set a standard no other girl in the school could match. But in 1999, it was a different story.

As we talked in my office, I could only lip-read about fifty percent of what she was saying. Her signing skills—actually her finger spelling skills, to be honest—added perhaps another thirty percent. The rest was purely fill-in-the-blanks guesswork on my part. It did take some effort, especially the lip-reading.

What the hell was I thinking?

I kept asking Melanie the same question over and over. It really bothered me because I had stumbled across a very sobering truth. In 1984, in my valiant effort to fit in with the mainstream, I was totally full of crap. I was Super Phony. I was telling the whole world, *hey, this is cool, I can fit in.* Telling everyone, *hey, don't worry, I communicate just fine with my hearing classmates.* Who was I kidding?

This is really nothing new. In fact, to some degree, I'd been aware of it all along. In my other book *Deaf Again,* I pointed out how I insisted that I fit in just fine with my hearing baseball teams, winning championships and all that. Yet when I joined the Gallaudet baseball team years later, I realized there was simply no comparison. With the Gallaudet team, I could not only communicate with my deaf teammates significantly more during the actual games, but also during locker room banter and on the bus during road trips.

With the aforementioned hearing teams, so many people marveled at how this brave deaf boy was able to fit in. Oh, baloney. I was Super Phony. In Cindy's case, I didn't realize it until just now: Super Phony had struck once again.

Don't get me wrong; I have nothing against hearing women. I also have nothing against my educational placement. Although getting through a hearing school was rather tricky, I still reaped the benefits of a wonderful academic program.

Instead, what I'm trying to do is shed light on an easy-to-overlook social phenomenon. It's the *Hey Ma, I fit in just fine with the hearing folk* lie that we often tell ourselves.

At first glance, many deaf people, myself included, are able to make it in the mainstream, sort of. We do it with mirrors, smokescreens, fake smiles, and lots of nodding. We are masters of tricking others into thinking all is fine and dandy. In many cases, we actually brainwash ourselves into thinking we've assimilated into the hearing world. Academically we may wind up learning our ABCs, but socially we are completely in the dark.

Furthermore, those of us with speech skills are real pros at convincing hearing teachers and parents that we fit in. Often, hearing parents will delude themselves by correlating speech ability with success in the hearing world.

But in my case, and in many others, appearances may not necessarily reflect the truth. For example, I may be able to speak but that doesn't take away from the fact that I am still deaf. I still can't understand what any group of hearing people are saying, unless they know sign language. Regardless, many people have said, *Oh, he speaks so well; he's just like any normal hearing person.*

The sad thing is many of us actually believe it, especially when we don't have a frame of reference. Which is why in 1984, I would have considered having ten children with Cindy—while today I understand she's a dear friend who, in spite of her many fine qualities, doesn't even come close to what Melanie has to offer.

The bottom line: For all we advocate on behalf of Deaf culture, it's a hard fact that mainstreaming and technological interventions (hearing aids, cochlear implants, etc.) are first options for many hearing parents of deaf children—hearing parents who have the right to choose whatever they want for their children regardless of how the deaf community feels.

It is not our place to criticize those who have done things differently than we would have. Rather, we can offer our support to those who are struggling to find themselves. I lived many years as Super Phony before finally discovering the deaf community. They welcomed me with open arms, allowing me to become more than I ever thought I could be. And that's the important thing.

Last but not least, I take it as my responsibility to keep the door open. There are countless other Super Phonies out there. Some may feel comfortable getting by in their environments. Others may look back and say the same thing I said:

What the hell was I thinking?

And when they say that, I'll only smile and welcome them—just like the rest of you have done for me. Thank you.

Millionaire School for the Deaf

"*H*oward," I wrote, "you hired a moron with a speech impediment to conduct celebrity interviews. Why not hire a deaf guy to take phone calls from your listeners?"

Yes, I had snapped. All of my better judgment went out the window and I did indeed send an inquiry to infamous shock jock Howard Stern, asking for a tryout on his radio show. After all, if he can work with Stuttering John Melendez, he can work with me. With my alter ego Deffman manning the phones, it would be a riot:

CALLER: I'd like to ask Howard for an autographed picture.

DEFFMAN: Eh? You want Howard to get on a giraffe with your sister?

See, I told you I'd snapped. What was I thinking?

Money. A truckload of money, that's what I was thinking. Because recent events have proven beyond a doubt that if you want to ride in a limo every day and own an island in the Caribbean, you need to be in the entertainment industry.

Think about it—as I write this article, Cleveland Indians outfielder Manny Ramirez and Seattle Mariners shortstop Alex Rodriguez are seeking multi-year contracts in excess of 200 million dollars. What do they do? They throw a ball. They catch a ball. They hit a ball. They spit. They scratch. Then they wheelbarrow a ton of money to the bank.

Meanwhile, thousands of bright, motivated college students go through several years of arduous study so that they may someday work in the school system, where they will offer much-needed educational, social-emotional support to children all over the country.

Without a doubt, schoolteachers are a valuable resource, molding today's kids into tomorrow's leaders. Unfortunately, once these teachers find gainful employment, their salary is usually in the neighborhood of thirty thousand dollars a year— about what A-Rod and Manny would make in one turn at-bat.

Not to pick on sports stars, mind you. It's just as bad in the movie industry. Bruce Willis and Arnold Schwarzenegger command millions of dollars per film. And it's a bummer to know that while they're making all that money shooting toy guns onscreen, there are plenty of teachers nationwide who have to deal with students packing REAL GUNS. Yippie-ki-yay *that*, Bruce. It just doesn't make sense.

But then again, this is America. No one said anything had to make sense. It's what makes our country so unique. So instead of griping about the injustice of it all, let's get with the program and get a piece of the action.

I humbly propose a formula to help create the world's first Millionaire School for the Deaf. Bear with me; I really believe we can do this. First and foremost, let's toss the ancient formula of ABCs and 123s out the window. If you've ever seen Pauly Shore or Buffy the Vampire Slayer, you should know by now that brains are not a prerequisite for a lucrative career. The secret, instead, is to be in the right place at the right time.

So here's what we do: set up a school for kids ages 2-18, but instead of the three R's, drill them exclusively in sports and entertainment. No topic is too outrageous. In addition to baseball, football, basketball, and the performing arts, you could also teach classes in Body Slamming 101 (hey, pro wrestling pays, big time). You could even offer a course in Presidential Nookie 201, where students learn how to seduce their way into the oval office—and consequently secure a multi-million dollar book deal. Gossip, as we all know, pays just as well as any other form of entertainment.

Of course, the odds of anyone becoming a pro athlete, movie star, wrestler, or presidential playmate are extremely remote. Which brings me to the second part of my plan: all families enrolling their children in the Millionaire School for the Deaf must sign a contract to participate in the Moolah Sharing Plan, or MSP.

The logic behind the MSP is the fact that regardless of the tough odds, the intensive training involved in our program increases the likelihood that sooner or later, someone is going to hit it big. And that someone will wind up getting a sports or movie contract worth more money than he or she will know what to do with.

Once that person hits it big, he will be obligated to turn over half of his windfall to the Millionaire School for the Deaf, as stipulated in the MSP. Yes, I'm serious.

Half of more money than you'd ever know what to do with is not much to ask. When A-Rod gets his 200 million dollars, for example, he will be filthy stinking rich. What would he be if he gave away half of it? Still filthy stinking rich. Catch my drift?

Assuming every now and then a Millionaire School for the Deaf student gets a lucrative sports or movie deal, he subsequently turns over half the money to his alma mater. The money would then be split evenly amongst school staff, students, and their families. Yes, the school would actually be paying families to send their kids there, not the other way around. Neat, huh? A couple of million could also be put aside in a special account designed to accrue a high percentage of interest, to cover the inevitable drought periods when no one hits the big time. Everyone would be filthy rich. Mo' money, mo' money...

All right, other than the obvious fact that I've lost my marbles, why am I writing this drivel? The truth is I work in the school system. No, I am not a teacher. I have it easy compared to teachers. But I work with teachers every day and I see them putting in thankless hours in their never-ending effort to make a difference in someone's life. They are overworked and underpaid, and to me that seems incredibly unfair. But they are indeed appreciated, and I wanted to take the time to say thank you. Teachers, you rock. You are the best.

I also wanted to take the time to slip in another message: Yoo-hoo, Howard, I'm waiting. Call me.

Editor's note: A-Rod eventually signed a 10-year, 250 million-dollar contract with the Texas Rangers. That strange thumping sound is Mark banging his head on the wall. And Howard never called.

Cochlear Controversy

*L*et's get this out of the way real quick. Let me say right now that I've never been too crazy about the cochlear implant. I personally have no interest in getting one. *Any* kind of surgery makes me nervous. Although I'm aware of claims that the earlier you get it the better, I still have mixed feelings about deaf kids getting a cochlear implant well before they're old enough to decide for themselves. At the same time, when older children and adults decide they want one, I have no objections. Whatever path a person deliberately chooses is his or her own business and no one else's.

Granted, I may be unfairly biased. My own experience with the pathological approach was extremely frustrating and repeatedly set me up for failure. In my eyes, all of the doctor visits, speech therapy, and hearing aids were a constant reminder of *what I was not.* I am not, and never will be, a hearing person. Only when people stopped trying to fix me did I finally learn how to focus on my strengths. Doing so was a tremendous boost that allowed me to make something out of my life. I know several other deaf people, including those who were implanted (against their own wishes), who have also shared similar stories of the "just let me be me" variety.

Recent events, however, have forced me to realize that maybe I need to re-evaluate the way I express my feelings about this sensitive topic. In both my personal life and at the '98 NAD conference, I had some experiences that really opened my eyes to a new phenomenon.

Not long ago I was the guest speaker at a parent workshop. The purpose of this workshop was to discuss many of the issues related to deafness that I wrote about in my first book, *Deaf Again*. One of the issues, of course, was the cochlear implant. My intention was to briefly tell the parents that I opposed it and to give a few examples that supported my views.

But before I could share my biased opinion, I recognized one of the parents in attendance. I knew who she was through an acquaintance of mine. This woman was the mother of a two-year-old deaf boy whom she already had implanted. This threw me off because I was accustomed to implantees being "out there," away from the deaf world.

Based on past experience, I've felt that most people who take a pathological view of deafness tend to ignore Deaf culture. It was always us against them. From opposing sides, it's easy to criticize one another.

Not so with this particular mother. She was a new breed. She took it upon herself to expose her deaf son to *everything*. She felt the implant had its advantages and that ASL had its advantages. She did not take the either/or path. Instead, she chose both.

So there she was, this mother of an implanted child, doing her best to learn everything she could about my world. She had every intention of fully immersing her son into Deaf culture, cochlear implant and all.

During my presentation, with this woman in attendance, I simply did not have the heart to share my feelings about the cochlear implant. The deed was done, her kid was hooked up, and it was time to move on. There was no point in me saying things that would make her feel miserable about a decision she could not reverse. I let it go.

Instead of talking negatively about the implant, I spoke positively about Deaf culture. All of the parents came out of it with a new understanding of the deaf world and I was satisfied.

Later, this woman found out that I had deliberately skipped over my anti-CI sentiments. Her reaction was "Mark, I wish you had gone ahead and told us how you really felt about it!" She really wanted to know. She valued the deaf perspective, warts and all. I cannot tell you enough how much I respect this. I also would like to say that if anyone gives her or her son a hard time because of his implant, they risk losing valuable future members of the deaf community.

Was this an isolated incident? No. There would be other implantees or parents of implantees interested in Deaf culture. This was messing with my head. Instead of us against them, it was them joining us. What else could I do but welcome them? If I were an arrogant bastard, I could thumb my nose at them and make Deaf culture look bad in the process.

Later on, at the '98 NAD conference in Texas, there was another experience that had me re-evaluating the way I go about my views. There was a workshop titled "Cochlear Implants and Deaf Adults: Implications for the Deaf Community from Within." On the panel were two culturally Deaf adults who decided to get the cochlear implant. Their goal was to show that it was possible for them to have the implant and still maintain their deaf identity.

In what was a fascinating session, Mary Pat Graham Kelly and Phil Aiello talked in depth about the cochlear implants they had chosen to get for themselves. They emphasized that their implants by no means took away their deaf identity (as Aiello insisted, "Hey, I'm still me"). A large audience watched attentively as Kelly and Aiello told their story and answered questions.

Kelly was initially raised as an oralist but learned about sign language through interpreters in college. She discovered they made life easier and fell in love with ASL. She met other culturally Deaf people and enjoyed socializing with the deaf community. As she said during her talk, "I truly found my deaf identity." At this point, she had no interest in cochlear implants.

Eventually, she met other deaf people who had the implant and decided to get one herself. She is happy with the results. She emphasized that she was, and still is, a member of the deaf community. She cautioned the audience not to have preconceived notions about those who have the implant, such as assuming they're oralists who don't accept Deaf culture. She closed her story by reiterating the importance of being sensitive to the needs of each individual

Aiello took the stage next and explained what had led him to get the implant. He had struggled with his decision, eventually deciding to go for it with hopes that it would help him in his business dealings with hearing customers (Aiello is Technical Director for Technical Computer Services). Not long before that very NAD conference, he went out and had the surgical procedure done. He marveled at the new sounds he was able to hear and had the audience howling with laughter when he joked about previously unknown noises emanating from the men's room.

On a more serious note, Aiello talked about the reaction of the deaf community. Most of his close friends asked him if he was sure he wanted the implant. Once he said yes, they supported his decision. It was easy to see who his real friends were. Other people gossiped behind his back, saying things such as "Oh, he wants to be hearing."

Aiello also acknowledged that the cochlear implant issue caused tension in his family when they wondered out loud if he really knew what he was getting himself into. He admitted that the implant will never make him hear at the same level as a hearing person, and that learning to use it will take lots of hard work. But he believes it will help him nonetheless, and his goal is to be able to speak to hearing customers on the phone. It is not our place to question his decision or commitment, for he did his own homework. He spoke to people who succeeded with the implant, and he spoke to people who failed with it. It was his call, no one else's, and I respect that.

Aiello also warned the crowd that "The deaf community must welcome people who have the cochlear implant. If you don't, you will get weaker." Aiello's point was well taken. It's obvious that if we don't accept him, that's one intelligent, powerful, and outspoken individual we'd lose right there. As Aiello and Kelly reminded us again, "It is possible for us and others to have the cochlear implant and still be members of the deaf community."

I won't lie to you. I still have mixed feelings about the cochlear implant. I still wonder if it's really appropriate for toddlers and young children. I still cringe when I hear about babies having cochlear implant surgery (or any surgery, for that matter). Yet if those same children and their parents choose to someday join the deaf world, we must welcome them. As for deaf adults, I have a new respect and understanding for those who have the cochlear implant. We all, as members of and role models for the deaf community, need to be open-minded about who we accept.

Whew, this article was heavy. At the next NAD conference I think I'll just cover the basket-weaving workshop.

The Impossible Ideal

After my recent *Cochlear Controversy* article, mayhem erupted everywhere. Especially in my own house. This is what happens when hearing relatives get their hands on stuff I've written. I am the family kook, the radical nitwit, and every now and then the folks like to check and see if my head is screwed on straight.

Basically, in the aforementioned article, I said that if an adult chooses to have a cochlear implant, that's his or her business. No one should complain about it. As for children, we could argue about this all day. Nonetheless, if a child already has an implant, it is imperative that the deaf community accepts this child.

Many children who do not succeed with the implant (and I have stated many times that it does not make Joe Deaf become Joe Hearing) eventually drift over to the deaf community. It's frustrating enough not to be able to fit in with the hearing world, and that would be compounded even more if a deaf child who failed with the implant later found himself rejected by the deaf community. So my stance, pure and simple, is: if someone already has a cochlear implant, let it go. Welcome that person.

Although for the most part I preached tolerance, I precluded that stuff with a disclaimer that my own personal opinion of the implant always has been, and still is, "No thanks." If you have or want a cochlear implant, that's fine with me. But I don't want one for myself.

This is where someone in my family took offense. Since Murphy's Law dictates this relative is somehow going to get his hands on this article, for sanity's sake (his and mine) I'm going to give him a fictional name. So, let's call him Jim Plante. (Jim Plante, implantee, get it?)

Jim definitely liked my article, particularly the way I showed acceptance for those who have the cochlear implant. But he did not like how I said I don't want one for myself. He also didn't agree with my concern about implanting young children before they are old enough to decide for themselves. He immediately challenged me to validate my opinion.

I explained how it was in the deaf world where I found professional success after years of frustration in the hearing world. After never quite measuring up to the hearing ideal, I discovered and thrived in Deaf culture. ASL opened far more doors for me than hearing aids or speech therapy ever did.

Jim, however, refused to acknowledge that Deaf culture exists. I objected and insisted that it did. The deaf world has its own language, arts, history, and mores, I explained. I showed him some materials from NAD and other deaf organizations, but he wouldn't budge from his perspective.

Taking one last shot, I tried to explain to Jim that Deaf culture is as important to me as Jewish culture is to him. How would he feel if mainstream society insisted he convert to the more prevalent Christian religions? Jim shook his head defiantly and bristled, "That's different!" Deaf culture, deaf schmulture, he said, I and every deaf person should jump at every opportunity to become more hearing. What better way to do this than get a cochlear implant? Jim truly believed this was the best way to go.

I felt exasperated. Rejected, even. For when Jim thumbs his nose at Deaf culture, he thumbs his nose at me. Deaf culture is who I am. It kind of stings when he rejects it.

Finally, Jim said our whole argument was moot anyway. Unbeknownst to me, he had recently attended a workshop on the cochlear implant and had actually asked the presenter if she thought I was a good candidate for it. Jim was disappointed to find out that I was not.

I was disappointed myself. Disappointed to learn that Jim still feels a need to go out and "fix" me. Okay, okay, I know he does it out of love. In his own way, he does what he thinks is best for me. Yet I wonder if he will ever see me as the successful deaf adult that I am. To him, I will always be the hearing impaired person in the family. The man who cannot hear. The man who needs to be repaired. The concept that I can survive, let alone thrive, in a world without sound is just too foreign to him. So he sets an ideal for me, an audist ideal that I cannot reach.

After all of the bickering that went on, I realized there was no way could I change Jim's views any more than he could have changed mine. We called it even. In spite of our different views, we still have a tremendous amount of love and respect for each other.

In retrospect, this was just an amusing argument between two individuals. But what do we, the deaf community, do as a whole to address this issue on a larger scale? The only thing I can think of is education and advocacy.

It's not uncommon, and in fact it's natural, for many hearing people to look at things from an entirely audist perspective. The world of ASL and Deaf culture is understandably incomprehensible to the average hearing guy. We're way out in left field. We need to do a better job of showing the hearing world that many of us are comfortable just the way we are, thank you very much.

If I may go off on a side note, it's also not uncommon for the deaf community to resist progress in medical technology, especially when it comes to the cochlear implant. Yes, that's me, guilty as charged. When we hear of cochlear implant failures, of which there are a considerable number, we are too quick to interpret this as license to say, "See, I told you." Yet, at the same time, there are a growing number of cochlear implant successes that we cannot ignore.

Essentially, my argument with Jim ended in a draw. We agreed to disagree. But I would have lost entirely if I did not have NAD and a strong organized deaf community to fall back on. For at one point in our argument, Jim insisted I had no proof. When I told him about the recent NAD conference, the many workshops, and research findings presented there, the many successful deaf adults who have succeeded on their own terms, Jim acknowledged it somewhat. But it was more like, "Yeah, yeah, whatever" and totally devoid of enthusiasm.

We quit yammering and instead joked to other relatives that we were going after each other's throats with our cochlear war. If anything, I think we spurred more discussion, more awareness, and hopefully more empathy regarding this sensitive topic.

In the meantime, Jim plans to show my original *Cochlear Controversy* article to other hearing relatives. I think I'm going to lock myself in the basement before they come after me.

Role Models

*T*he VCR alert was on. Several friends, relatives, and people on Internet mailing lists had informed me that NBC's *Dateline* was going to run a feature on the cochlear implant. As always, the rumors and speculations were rampant. Would the news feature be biased in favor of or against the implant? Would they show just the feel-good success stories, sweeping the failures under the rug? Would this be one of those reports that focused entirely on the ear, and not the whole person? Would it just be medical professionals saying, "See, we can fix them," or would culturally Deaf people be given an opportunity to share a deaf perspective?

I eagerly awaited the *Dateline* segment, which I soon learned was going to focus on an adorable young girl's success with her cochlear implant. For the most part, the feature was pretty much what I had expected. It celebrated a family's joy after their daughter's hearing improved with the implant, and *Dateline* covered all the bases by showing both sides of the cochlear controversy. But it was the same old pro and con arguments, the ones I've seen and debated a zillion times.

Perhaps the story was a miraculous inspiration to those who look to the cochlear implant as a beacon of hope. Perhaps it raised the ire of those who oppose it. For me, it was same old, same old. The debate rages on, but I've been through the mill a few too many times.

It was not the cochlear implant feature that had me talking to everyone the next day. Instead, it was the story that came on right before, one that focused on a paralyzed bike racer. Now *that* was the story that really caught my attention and tugged at my heartstrings. It had a message everyone needs to be aware of.

The story was about a man named David Bailey, who was the number one motocross racer in the country before a practice-run accident paralyzed him from the waist down. As the feature went on, Bailey acknowledged how his life hit rock bottom after the accident. Such was his despair that at one point he even became suicidal.

Fortunately, fate intervened and Bailey got to meet Jim Knaub, a wheelchair marathon champ. Knaub inspired Bailey to become a wheelchair racer and the two of them trained together. Knaub persistently challenged Bailey, refusing to let him get down on himself.

Eventually, an amazing transformation took place. Not only did Bailey discover he could still be a world-class athlete, but he even entered an ironman competition. It was one of the most fascinating comeback stories I have ever seen.

While watching this story with my wife, I asked her if she noticed a parallel, a recurring theme. After all, Bailey was in the pits until he met someone exactly like himself. Sound familiar?

Yes, my wife and I—and countless other deaf people—kind of stumbled along with our deafness until we met other successful deaf role models. Role models who kicked us in the butt and inspired us to do more. I cannot emphasize enough how important this is. Role models, role models. They lay the foundation for success.

It was a deaf person in Kamloops, British Columbia, who inspired my wife to change her life for the better. She was encouraged to attend Gallaudet University and get an advanced degree in education, which she did. Likewise, it took two Deaf Ph.D.s at Gallaudet to kick me in the rear and help me understand that I could accomplish more than I ever gave myself credit for.

This is why I have repeatedly mentioned the importance of deaf children getting the opportunity to interact with deaf peers and adults. I have written about this many times in past articles and will continue to do so in future articles until my fingernails fall off.

It still concerns me how many people, in their efforts to normalize deaf children, insist on shielding them from the deaf community. Yes, the goal is to succeed in the mainstream and that's an admirable goal in itself. But again, many people find strength and support from their true peers; that's what I believe allows them to take off and succeed anywhere else.

And that, my dear readers, is the moral of the story. Whoever you are, whatever you believe in, one of the healthiest things you can do is meet other people who have been in the same boat as you.

Role models, role models. They are priceless.

Techno-Nerds

*T*he three of us just stood there, smack in the middle of a hotel parking lot. Each of us had one arm outstretched towards the sky. We surrounded the antenna of a hotel van while gripping a strange-looking device. There was no shortage of weird looks as hotel guests walked by. All right, let's take a quick quiz. The three of us were:

A) Doing an impersonation of the Statue of Liberty.

B) Starfleet Officers searching for signs of intelligent life.

C) Research specialists running lab tests for a new underarm deodorant.

D) Three idiots desperately trying to get a signal on their 2-way pagers.

If you picked "D," congratulations. You win a weekend in a good old-fashioned, technology-free home (more details at the end

111

of this article). Because yes, that was me and two other friends in the Genetti Hotel parking lot desperately trying our best to squeeze messages out of our beloved pagers.

We were at the Pennsylvania Society for Advancement of the Deaf's annual convention in Williamsport, Pennsylvania. It's a beautiful town situated in... uh...um... well, quite frankly, the middle of nowhere. It's a small town surrounded by mountains that effectively blocked all transmission from our pagers.

One of us somehow got the idea that by holding our pagers up against a radio antenna, we could get a transmitter boost strong enough to send or receive a few messages.

So there I was, standing there like a moron, arm held up high with my pager pressed against the antenna of an old van. That's when it hit me: I was a dweeb, a nerd, and a technology addict. It was time to get a life. Couldn't I live for a few days without the constant bombardment of pager and e-mail messages? What was I thinking?

Most messages are work related and the personal ones are usually my wife saying "Honey, pick up some eggs on the way home." Couldn't I just turn off the danged thing, lock it up in my suitcase, and leave well enough alone?

No, I couldn't. With the pager a dud, I went to the hotel lobby and requested a TDD. Call it a guilt trip or a technology addiction, but I just had to let the folks at home know that I had no pager access. The clerk handed me a tiny TDD that looked more like a calculator. On top of that, the battery was dead.

Unable to use the pay phone, I had to go upstairs to my room where I could plug the TDD into an outlet. The phone was on a tiny desk in between twin beds and it was so cramped that I had to get down on my knees and hunch over the phone in order to make the call.

As I was calling home, the maid walked in. She saw me on my knees and gasped. She apologized profusely as she made a hasty retreat. I can only imagine what was going on in her mind. Either she thought I was a religious fanatic praying to the Great Lord of the TDD, or perhaps I was an FBI agent sending top-secret messages to Washington.

That's when I decided the technology had to go. I returned the TDD, put my pager away, and wound up having a great time without them.

That brings us back to your prize: your free weekend in a technology-free home. To get there, just pull the plug out from every device in your house. Unplug the TV, the telephone, and the computer. Turn off your pager and put it away. Curl up with a nice book and a cold drink, and there you go. You'll thank me later.

The Gentle Art of Deflection

Seventeen-year-old Darla is enjoying her meal at the dinner table, when suddenly she drops a bombshell.

"Mom, dad..." she begins. "I'm going to turn down the scholarship to Harvard and spend the year hitchhiking through the country. I need to find myself."

Darla's two brothers, Larry and Mike, freeze on the spot. Mom has already fainted and dad is about to go ballistic. The veins are popping on his forehead, a clear indication of the explosive tirade everyone knows is coming.

"Coffee, anyone?" interjects a smiling Aunt Thelma, breaking the tension. "Such a wonderful dinner, we'd love to end it with some fresh coffee... wouldn't we?"

Such deflective interruptions are more common than we might think. In fact, they happen all the time on TV sitcoms. It works like this: Aunt Joy admits she's having an affair. Uncle Joey demands a divorce. The dog is humping Aunt Madeline's leg. For what feels like an eternity, there's an awkward moment of silence. Then, out of the blue, someone says:

"Hey, this soup is delicious, isn't it?"

These off-the-point diversions serve their purpose well. They break the tension and send the conversation off in a different direction. It's a verbal way of sticking one's head in the sand. In a nutshell, it's the gentle art of deflection.

This verbal self-defense technique is practiced, on an advanced level, in many situations where a deaf person is surrounded by friends and relatives who don't sign.

Let's say, for example, Cousin Harry tells that joke about the traveling salesman and the room erupts in laughter. Except, of course, for deaf Grandpa Joe who missed the joke. Aunt Millie might notice that Grandpa Joe isn't laughing, and since she can't sign fluently enough to relay the joke, she instead says:

"Here, have another meatball sandwich." Mission accomplished, awkward moment deflected.

Sometimes it's the deaf person himself who does the deflecting. Suppose, for example, Grandpa Joe was aware of all the hearing people laughing. Perhaps he not only doesn't want to feel like the odd man out, but he also doesn't want to be the object of pity. At this juncture, Grandpa Joe may choose to deflect attention away from himself.

The first strategy could be a simple, well-timed smile. That way when everyone else was cracking up, Grandpa Joe wouldn't stick out like a sore thumb. Another strategy could be to reach for the same props Aunt Millie used. He could grab a sandwich and stuff his face, covering up the fact that he doesn't have the slightest idea what anyone is talking about. Or, better yet, he could just excuse himself and go watch the football game on TV. Who could blame him? Last but not least, he could do double duty as a busboy. Clear the table, wash the dishes, and serve dessert. He'd still be as lost as ever, but hey, he'd look busy.

Great ideas, aren't they? No? I didn't think so, either. But we've all been guilty of playing the deflection game to one extent or the other. Maybe it's time to stop. In fact, next time there's raucous laughter in the room, maintain a poker face and say the four magic words:

"What did he say?"

Go on; try it. You'll be amazed at the results. Granted, it's not easy to do. Sometimes it's easier to keep the peace than to face the truth. Truth hurts. It takes a tremendous amount of courage to stand up and just say, *"Hey, I'm deaf as a post and I don't understand a word anyone is saying. What can we do about it?"* But you can do it. That's right, throw all caution to the wind, and walk through the fire.

The uneasiness and awkwardness coming from such straightforwardness may no doubt send Aunt Millie scurrying for another meatball sandwich. Nonetheless, hang in there. Sometimes chaos is healthy. When the smoke clears, everything can be rebuilt from a more solid foundation.

My family tried it and the results were nothing short of miraculous. We now have an ASL interpreter at all major family events and holidays. A few relatives have signed up for ASL classes. The younger kids in the family have noticed this and are becoming interested in ASL themselves. Speaking up was deafinitely worth it.

So if you're one of those kind souls trying to keep the peace by hiding behind a meatball sandwich, bless you. You're too nice. But just once, try letting the truth come out and see what happens. Good luck!

The Return of Super Phony

What's that thing up there in the sky? It's flying around aimlessly. It's totally lost. It's a bird, it's a plane, it's a guy nodding his head. Oh, no. It can't be. Yes, it's *Super Phony!*

Nodding faster than a Sammy Sosa bobblehead doll, deftly fooling thousands of unsuspecting hearing people, Super Phony's biggest weapons are the word "yes" and a charming smile capable of deceiving anyone.

Super Phony's amazing powers were harnessed in the early '70s. Surrounded by hearing classmates and teachers, he realized that hearing loss was not in vogue. It was cool to wear platform shoes and bell-bottom pants, but not a hearing aid. He needed to fit in.

Fitting in took a tremendous amount of skill. Sitting up front. Reading lips. Pretending to take notes. Smiling or laughing at the precise moment that hearing people smiled or laughed. Being careful not to ask others to repeat things too often. And, above all, nodding and saying "yes" to the most incomprehensible questions.

117

In the '80s, our hapless friend made the jump to superhero status. As did Spiderman, Super Phony emerged from a mishap in a science lab. While a radioactive spider bit Peter Parker, Super Phony got zapped by a high school chemistry teacher.

A double major in science, Super Phony had already completed a physics project for the annual science fair. Meanwhile, he didn't bother setting up a display for his chemistry class, thinking it was an optional assignment. It was only two days before the big event when he realized the error of his ways.

"You mean we *have* to do this?" Super Phony asked Erik, a fellow classmate.

"Didn't you get the assignment?" Erik responded. "Mrs. Williams asked you to do it two months ago. I could have sworn you said yes."

Super Phony smacked himself on the head. "I only said yes to get out of her office. I never had a clue what she was talking about. Oh, man. Mighty fine mess we're in."

"We?" asked Erik. "What do you mean, we?"

Super Phony flashed a mischievous smile. "Yeah, we. We're going to make this work. I'm going to need you, Steven, Matt..."

Two days later, a true superhero was born. Faster than a speeding bullet, able to jump over a building in a single bound, and dumb as a plank. Super Phony proudly took his position next to his physics display on the third floor. The chemistry exhibit was on the second floor, as was Mrs. Williams. But when she took a break and headed upstairs, a sophisticated escape plan went into effect.

"Red alert!" signaled Erik. Super Phony immediately ducked under a table, crawled out the other end, and headed down the corridor with his comrade. He was immediately replaced at the physics display by Steven, who took over Super Phony's presentation without missing a beat.

Laying low on the second floor, Super Phony was out of danger for the time being. Until...

"Duck!" He was grabbed from behind by Matt, who quickly pulled him into the boys' bathroom. One second later Mrs. Williams walked by, totally oblivious to the perfectly synchronized evasive maneuvers of Team Super Phony.

For the next two hours, Operation Duck Williams was a tremendous success. Super Phony was a bona fide hero. His physics presentation went off without a hitch. His sidekicks managed to keep him under Mrs. William's radar. He appeared and disappeared at will. And, oh yes, he also got a big fat "zero" on his chemistry project.

There would be more Super Phony incidents in the years to come. But when Super Phony enrolled at Gallaudet University his powers suddenly went dormant. He could actually understand what people were saying. There was no need to resort to heroic acts of extreme fakery. He was finally a real person.

Yes, I was Super Phony. I have hung up my cape and no longer play these games. Or do I?

A few years later, I went to a deli and ordered a tuna salad hoagie. The deli guy responded with a question. I didn't fully understand him but thought he repeated "tuna salad hoagie" just to confirm my order. I smiled and said "yes."

He went ahead and put together something that

did not appear to be what I ordered. Oh, someone else was in line before me, I figured. The deli guy made a few friendly comments as I waited, and I smiled right back. He then handed me two Italian hoagies. Go ahead, say it three times fast with a deaf voice: tuna salad hoagie, two Italian hoagies.

I took the Italian hoagies and smiled. I felt a sudden surge of phoniness. Could it be? Yes. My powers were baaaaaaaack.

On The Fence

*A*fter writing countless deaf-related articles, I recently received an e-mail from a woman who told me I often overlooked a certain group. The deaf stuff was nice, she said. But what about the hard of hearing, particularly those who are stuck in between? The ones "on the fence," not quite hearing enough to fit into the hearing world and not quite deaf enough to fit into the deaf world? She had a good point. I hadn't given it much thought because lately I've pretty much immersed myself in the deaf community. Nonetheless, there was a time when I was in limbo. This article is for those of you who still are.

First of all, if you were born deaf/hard of hearing (or become deaf/HOH later in life), I'm sorry to say that you will never completely fit into the hearing world, period. That's it, that's a hardcore fact that will never change. Sure, you can assimilate into the hearing world with varying degrees of success, but only to a certain degree. Residual hearing, lip-reading skills, and technological devices may certainly help. But again, only to a certain degree. You will never completely fit in 100 percent.

Some of us can put on an Oscar performance where we give the impression we're doing just fine with the hearing folks. I used to do this all the time. I was a master at it. One-on-one conversations with hearing people were usually a breeze, so long as the person speaking didn't have a walrus mustache or an icky gob of spinach stuck between his teeth. Two-on-one took some more effort, but I could fill in the blanks and make it work. Groups, on the other hand, were much harder.

Sometimes I could lip-read just enough to figure out what the topic was in a group conversation. But to understand everything was impossible. Even if I had the right balance of residual hearing and lip-reading skills, to use them in group situations is very exhausting.

In my opinion, it's asking too much. It's easier to just pretend you know what's going on than to actually try to keep up. I could get away with making a few rounds of one-on-one, smiling in general, and looking like I was content. I did this in high school and in various employment settings in the hearing world. I felt it was necessary because I was under the impression that it was my responsibility to fit in. To object to anything, to demand that other people meet me halfway, would have been rocking the boat. It was, as so many people reminded me, a hearing world. (It would take me a while to learn that there is indeed a halfway: interpreters, relay services, assistive devices, and so on. But that's another story.)

So when I finally joined the deaf community, it must have been a piece of cake, a tremendous relief, right? Not exactly. Although I have a number of deaf relatives who use sign language, my own signing skills were rusty when I finally joined their world of Deaf culture. Having been postlingually deaf, I was encouraged to stick with the good speech and eschew the sign language. Strange but true. The end result was that although my receptive skills were pretty good from watching deaf relatives sign to each other, my own signing was more like Signed Exact English as opposed to the ASL most culturally Deaf people use.

My first true involvement with the deaf community was a dorm counseling job in 1988 at the Pennsylvania School for the Deaf. Great experience, yes, but initially I didn't consider that a full immersion into Deaf culture. A lot of the staff were hearing people who signed the same way I did (pretty clearly, but not fully ASL), and the truly deaf staff didn't really socialize with me that much. I actually felt like I had more in common with the hearing staff. The deaf staff signed so fluently; I felt I didn't belong with them.

During a holiday party, one deaf person jokingly told me not to worry about it because I was still "hearing-minded" (signing "hearing" over the forehead), and that I would learn more in due time. She was right, and she was only trying to help, but that comment bothered me. I realized right there that as much as I didn't fit into the hearing world, I didn't fit into the deaf world, either.

To address this problem head-on, I joined a local deaf club. Fun? Yes. Easy? No. On one hand, there was the thrill of understanding a lot more of what people were saying. At hearing clubs, forget it, I was always completely lost. In the deaf club, I had significantly more access. It was quite a breath of fresh air.

On the other hand, it was still somewhat of a struggle getting acclimated to my new deaf environment. Those who were native ASLers completely blew me away with their rapid signing. Their hands were flying all over the place, too fast for me to comprehend. Was I incompetent or what? After all, there I was, deaf myself, unable to follow the best signers.

To make matters worse, some of those native ASLers had a low tolerance for newbies like me. Some of them were willing to adjust their signing to accommodate me, while others brushed me off. One guy got me real good with a practical joke: I asked him what the sign was for a certain drink, and he gave me the sign for "idiot." Sucker that I was, I went up to the bartender to place my order.

> *"What do you want?" asked the bartender.*
> *"Idiot, me," I responded in ASL.*
> *"Yeah, I know you're an idiot, but what do you want to drink?"*

Obviously, the first thing I learned about the deaf world was that it had a sense of humor. It wasn't so bad, really. With time and perseverance, I gradually became a part of it in a way I never could with the hearing world. Any deaf person, given a reasonable amount of time, can sufficiently learn how to use sign language. I have never seen a deaf person learn how to hear and use it perfectly in the hearing world, yet I know of countless deaf people who found their niche in the deaf world.

Granted, there are those who remain on the fence and just don't feel much of a connection to the deaf world. This is understandable. For example, during all those years in a hearing high school, English alone was my primary language. ASL, as we all know, is a completely different language with a completely different syntax. So if you're joining Deaf culture late, it's not unusual to experience culture shock.

On many occasions in the deaf world, I would sign (in English word order) a hearing idiom and be greeted with blank stares. Conversely, someone might throw me an ASL idiom, a sign or signed phrase which had no English equivalent, and I'd be confused. It took me a long while to adjust, and I can see very well why some of those who are on the fence might feel like they're in a completely different world: they are.

Is there any solution to this uncomfortable limbo of not quite fitting in here and not quite fitting in there? That depends on individual preference. I had two strategies that helped me adjust to the deaf world:

Number one: Find others who are going through the same thing you are. In other words, the best way for people on the fence to find comfort is to find other people who are on the fence. During my early years as a member of a deaf organization, I found other deaf/HOH people who were also relatively new to the scene. We had a lot in common and were able to offer each other a lot of support. In due time, we all became a part of the deaf community and I'm grateful for the experience.

Number two: Find a mentor in the deaf community. It helps to have a special friend who is culturally Deaf yet sensitive to your needs as a New Deafie. In my case, it was my friend Vijay who was (and still is) a fantastic friend and mentor. There were some things in the deaf world that were very frustrating at the time, and I might have given up on it were it not for Vijay.

Of course, I realize that my answers may not be for everyone. They are what worked exclusively for me. It must be acknowledged that there are still a lot of deaf people who just don't feel comfortable in Deaf culture, and no one should force them along. In this case, the answer is similar to my first solution: find your peers, whoever they may be. If you consider yourself hard of hearing, if you don't really like signing that much, keep in mind that there are many deaf people who feel the same way. Find them. The worse thing about being on the fence, in my opinion, is the feeling that you are alone. Whoever you are, whatever you believe in, I hope you find your answers. Above all, be true to yourself.

Ooh, My Back

*Q*uick, tense your shoulders. Lift them an inch or two higher than normal. Hold this tension for about 15 seconds, then let go. Ahhhh, nice, isn't it? Now tense them again. This time, stick your head forward at an awkward angle and squint. Hold this position for, say, 35 years. Welcome to the world of the hard of hearing.

I never realized being hard of hearing was so exhausting. As a culturally Deaf person I've had the luxury of understanding my signing friends and relatives with minimal effort. Likewise, there are countless hearing people who can easily hold a conversation without even looking at each other. Yet for the hard of hearing, it can be an entirely different story, one I'd completely forgotten.

Yes, there once was a time when I was not quite hearing and not quite deaf. Spoken English was my language of choice for many years, but that was so long ago. It wasn't until a mental health professionals' workshop in the spring of 2002 when someone took me back to those lost years of "Eh? Whazzat?"

Dr. Samuel Trychin, hard of hearing himself, gave a fascinating keynote address. He shared several anecdotes about the hard of hearing experience, including a few hilarious misunderstandings that had everyone chuckling. But as Dr. Trychin pointed out, it was not entirely a laughing matter.

Included in the daily grind of being hard of hearing are some not so funny physical and emotional symptoms. The mental stress of constantly trying to keep up with what people are saying can bring forth some very real problems such as muscle tension, fatigue, high blood pressure, anxiety, irritability, and much more.

As I soaked up all of this information, I suddenly recalled those dreaded days when I had to sit up front, read lips, wear my hearing aid, and still make a fool out of myself with misunderstandings galore.

"Holy smokes," I said to a friend sitting next to me. "I'm a recovering HOH!" We laughed but didn't think much about it afterwards.

Then, three months later, I blew out my back lifting heavy furniture. To my relief, an MRI indicated it was not a severe injury. A follow-up evaluation with a physical therapist revealed unusual tightness in the muscles supporting my back. This, more than the heavy furniture, was what caused the trouble. It was like a tight rubber band just about ready to snap, an accident waiting to happen. The heavy lifting simply pushed it over the edge.

Soon afterwards I came across an intriguing book called *Healing Back Pain* by Dr. John Sarno. He insists that a great majority of back problems, save for the rare few serious conditions, are a result of being under too much stress. He even has a name for it: Tension Myositis Syndrome. It often occurs between the ages of 30 and 60, also known as the years of responsibility.

In a nutshell, stubborn morons like me are too proud to admit we're overwhelmed. Instead it is much easier to go "Ooh, my back!" and chill out on the Barcalounger. In my house, "Ooh, my back!" can often be heard around 1:00 on any given Sunday— just in time for the opening kickoff.

Seriously, Dr. Sarno's book clearly demonstrates how a lot of our emotional stress is suppressed and consequently emerges in other ways. Namely, back pain. Among the symptoms of TMS are muscle tension, fatigue, high blood pressure, anxiety, irritability, and... waitaminute! Where have we seen this before?

Upon reading Dr. Sarno's findings, I immediately dug up an old transcript of Dr. Trychin's presentation. The physical symptoms of the hard of hearing and of Tension Myositis Syndrome were practically identical. Eureka! I think I just discovered Hard of Hearing Tension Myositis Syndrome.

It makes sense, it really does. Dr. Sarno says our daily stress is a factor in back pain; Dr. Trychin indicates "chronic muscle tension" comes with the territory for the hard of hearing. Dr. Sarno reveals that the try-to-please-everyone personality type tends to get TMS, while Dr. Trychin describes some hard of hearing people as "overfunctioning" and feeling "totally responsible for communication." The parallel between these two guys is uncanny.

Therefore, if you are hard of hearing and you have some kind of back or neck pain, I strongly suggest reading up on both Dr. Trychin and Dr. Sarno. And, as both of them suggest, you could benefit from an attitude overhaul.

Face it: you are who you are. If other people have a problem with it, tough cookies. As Dr. Trychin observes, a lot of hard of hearing people place the burden on themselves. The truth is, communication is a two way street. Understand this, and don't kick yourself in the butt when Mr. Walrus Mustache mumbles something you can't understand. Other people need to meet you halfway. If they don't, they're not worth your time.

Even though the focus of this article is on the hard of hearing, I don't think deaf people are immune to Hard of Hearing Tension Myositis Syndrome. Many deaf people have grown up in families where few or no people sign. Many have been pressured into accepting a communication method that is not comfortable for them.

Either way, deaf or hard of hearing, it's time you start being nice to yourself. Loosen up and get yourself to the gym or a health spa (Note: As with any exercise program, check with your doctor before you start). Get a massage, jump in the hot tub, or burn off stress by hitting the weights. Any form of exercise and relaxation training will do you good.

Well, I'm cured now. I never knew that my school days of sitting up front, hunching my shoulders, reading lips, and trying to fit in with the hearing folks would cause my back to go kablooey several years later. But again, I'm fine. Wish I could stay, but here comes the wife asking me to get off the computer and throw out the trash.

Ooh, my back...

Editor's note: This article was originally published December 2002 in the National Association of the Deaf's Members Only *website.*

Drive Me Crazy at Below Invoice

Buying a new car can be a tremendous thrill. That new car smell, custom features, and all of the latest technological gizmos can have you drooling all over yourself.

Unfortunately, it's not all fun and games. Negotiating with dealerships is tricky and it's hard to know if you're really getting a good deal. But with some patience and common sense, you can turn things around in your favor.

Recently, I shopped for a minivan and it was an exhausting process. But once I realized what the salesmen were doing, I started having some fun.

The minute I pulled into the parking lot of Piranhas-R-Us, a salesman was right in my face. My wife and I were only looking but he still managed to get us inside to talk numbers. Dang, he was good.

"If I could sell you this minivan for only $100 over invoice, would you buy it now?" He asked. I said I didn't know.

"Don't you think that's a fair price?" the nice man asked.

"I don't know," I repeated. "It depends on what the dealership actually paid for it." Mr. Piranha frowned. He got up and was soon replaced by Mr. Assistant Piranha. This is what's known as a turn over. The idea is that by repeatedly switching like tag-team wrestlers, the sales team can wear you down.

What do you do in a situation like this? One option is to just leave—don't let them play with you. But I'm weird—I like to play along with them. I utilized my own turn over system, having my wife come in and replace me. We had our three-year-old son with us and we took turns looking after him— so anytime we got T.O.'ed, we T.O.'ed right back. They were not amused. My wife and I, on the other hand, were thoroughly enjoying ourselves.

Another thing we did was become deafer than ever. If you are hard of hearing and/or can use your voice, stop. In a car dealership, be stone deaf. Make them write everything down. Do this twenty minutes before closing time, and in their rush to make a sale they'll usually drop the price a lot faster.

On one hand, it worked. These tag team buddies were now offering a minivan at what they said was $500 below invoice. Then again, I knew of another dealership that started negotiations at that very same price, so I wasn't budging. I knew it could go lower.

On top of that, these guys were real professionals. They were using my "write everything down" ploy against me. When they asked why I still wasn't committing to a sale, I stupidly gave them a reason— at which point they jumped on something I previously wrote.

"But you said..." they pointed to the paper. Dang, real impressive. They were now using my own words against me in an effort to confuse me with my own logic.

"I'm schizophrenic," I quipped. "I'm allowed to change my mind and my personality every two minutes." Again, they were not amused. But my mind was made up: if we were going to play with my money, we were going to play by my rules.

They lowered their offer a bit more, but told me they'd need the manager's approval. One of them took a piece of paper to a guy in the back, who for all I knew could have been the janitor. He grabbed the paper, ripped it up, and screamed at the salesman.

Where was the popcorn? This was a great show. Most likely it was an act, designed to get me to say, "Wow, this must be a good deal. Look how mad the manager is. I better grab it while I can." Even if it wasn't an act, such behavior confirmed that these were people I didn't want to be dealing with.

At that point I wrote down their best offer and started to leave, saying maybe I'd be back after some more comparison-shopping.

"Waitaminute," said one of the salesmen. "If I can get you *this* price, right now, would you..." I cut him off. Let me tell you now: never get sucked into the manipulative "If I can, would you" game. Instead, respond like I did:

"If you were me, would you make a $20,000 decision in only five minutes, just to please some salesman you don't really know and will never see again?"

The salesman smiled in resignation and shook my hand. My family left the premises and we wound up finding a much better deal somewhere else.

Granted, not all car dealerships are this bad. I just happened to walk into a place that used a high-pressure system and I recommend avoiding those.

Either way, it's still a business and you need to be prepared for it. It's not the salesman's job to let you know you could get a better deal; it's entirely up to you to find one. Check your local bookstore, find a few guidebooks on how to buy a car, and do your homework. You'll be glad you did.

Editor's note: Mark credits Remar Sutton's Don't Get Taken Every Time *for arming him with the strategy to maneuver around Piranhas-R-Us. Without Sutton's book, this article doesn't happen and Mark's wallet is significantly lighter.*

Captioned Films &
Spastic Mailboxes

I did it again. I stuck my nose in an Internet chat room and wound up yakking all night long. It was a deaf discussion group and we covered every topic imaginable. Communication philosophies, the latest news, deaf events, you name it. It's all there, a mouse-click away. Technology sure has come along, hasn't it? I'm just not so sure if it's as wonderful as we think it is.

When I joined the latest deaf chat room, I instantly made a number of friends from all over the world. It was at that moment when I realized I now have more friends lurking in the dark recesses of my computer than I do in my own neighborhood. (You know, the one where I actually socialize with people face to face.) What do I call these friends on the Internet? Virtual friends? E-friends? Granted, these are indeed very real people discussing very real issues, and they are indeed pretty nice folks.

But it's starting to feel weird. By typing on a keyboard and clicking a mouse, I'm meeting people all over the world much faster than I ever could if I got off my lazy butt and actually went out to meet them. It makes me wonder about the very nature of technology. It's simultaneously a blessing and a curse.

When I was a kid, way back when toys didn't need batteries or microchips, life was much simpler. It had to be lived, out there. Yes, outside the safe confines of my house. There wasn't any captioned TV back when I was growing up so I had no choice but to go outside and play. I would usually play baseball with my friends all day long during the summer months. If we weren't playing baseball, we were at least doing something that required a lot of activity and imagination.

Also, prior to the advent of closed-captions, the only way to see a captioned show was to send for those government-sponsored captioned movies. Someone in the deaf community who owned a movie projector would order these open-captioned films and everyone would get together to watch them. My favorite memories are of the old James Bond movies starring Sean Connery. They weren't just movies, they were community events.

Today, most deaf families stay home with their captioned TVs, VCRs and DVDs. Generally, this is a great development. Widespread captioning allows deaf people to have access to news media, popular TV shows, the latest video/DVD releases, and so on. An added bonus is that all this captioning access helps many deaf people, especially children, to improve their reading skills. Overall, it's fantastic. But I will never forget the good old days when James Bond was a big event. I guess I'm just a nostalgic old dinosaur at heart.

TTYs are another story. When I was growing

up, there were no TTYs and no relay service. Because of this, my deaf parents and I became overly dependent on hearing people for even the most routine phone calls.

As for important phone calls, my parents and I were helpless bystanders as hearing relatives took over the lines. Sometimes, they dominated phone conversations that were meant for us, such as a teacher calling to inform my parents that I'd been firing spitballs in class again. For situations like this, and others of a more serious nature, my deaf parents were left out of the loop. At best, the teacher would talk for a long time and a hearing relative would nod "uh-huh, uh-huh, uh-huh," while my parents were going crazy trying to figure out what was going on. When they asked, they'd get a quick "waitaminute," followed much later by a one-sentence summary of a ten-minute conversation.

Also, deaf people obviously didn't have the luxury of calling each other. The only choices were to mail a letter, make an unannounced visit, or go bug a hearing neighbor to call your deaf friend's hearing neighbor. This was always a hassle because even if you got your neighbor to reluctantly step away from her favorite TV show, you still had to hope that your friend's neighbor and your friend himself were also home at that very moment.

On top of that, even if all this went off without a hitch, it was not uncommon for the hearing neighbors to go off on their own side conversations, or do their own editing of what was supposed to be your phone call. Which, of course, meant more "uh-huh, uh-huh, uh-huh," and "waitaminute" for the poor deaf schmuck helplessly standing there.

Last but not least, pity on the poor soul who had to make a private call to the doctor:

NEIGHBOR: "Doc, I got my deaf neighbor Joey right here. Just a second..."
JOEY: (gesturing)
NEIGHBOR: "He says he has a serious case of bellybutton lint."
JOEY: (gesturing)
NEIGHBOR: "And he has this strange fungus growing in his armpits."
JOEY: (gesturing)
NEIGHBOR: (listening to doctor) "Uh-huh, uh-huh..."
JOEY: "What did he say? What did he say?"
NEIGHBOR: "Uh-huh, uh-huh..."
JOEY: "What did he say?"
NEIGHBOR (lifting one finger and telling Joey to wait): "Uh-huh, uh-huh..."
JOEY: "Come on!"
NEIGHBOR: "Uh-huh... yes, mighty nasty weather we've had lately..."
JOEY: (gives up and grumbles on his way to another neighbor's house)

Nuts, isn't it? I'm sure glad that today we can make our own phone calls. But if there was one positive result from all that limited access in the past, it was the fact that deaf clubs were absolutely packed to capacity most weekends. This was our chance to catch up on all the news we weren't able to share with each other over the phone.

And then, hallelujah, the TTY was invented. I remember my first TTY like it was yesterday. How could I forget? That big old clunker looked like a spastic mailbox, shaking and humming as it printed out every conversation. It must have weighed a ton. It used up rolls of paper and was so noisy the cat would scurry under the bed every time I got a phone call.

Today, on the other hand, I have my nice little ultra-compact supercom. It's light as a feather. It has a nice digital screen, a built-in answering machine, and a memory that allows me to replay conversations.

This fantastic device, however, is also becoming obsolete as my computer now handles e-mail and fax, not to mention the usual online services that make it possible to chat with people all over the world. Also, let's not forget two-way pagers, which have turned deaf people into the equivalent of those annoying hearing folks who are always yapping into a cell phone.

All in all, the technological advances have been great. I shouldn't complain. In fact, I'm conveniently e-mailing this very article to my editor as soon as it's done. Right after I've finished this piece, it will travel cross-country and appear on someone else's screen in the blink of an eye. One can't argue with that. I guess technology really has improved the way society functions. But if you will excuse me, I think I'll step outside and see if society is still out there in person. See ya later!

Editor's note: This article was originally published March 2003 in the National Association of the Deaf's Members Only *website.*

The Timeless Argument

*F*or years, centuries even, the conflict has raged on. People have debated endlessly over which is better: sign language or speech. They're still going at it. As the argument evolved over the years it essentially proved that the more things change, the more they stay the same.

In addition to the timeless oral vs. manual debate, new topics have been added to the mix. Residential schools vs. mainstreaming. The validity of Deaf culture. Educational approaches such as the Bi-Bi philosophy. The cochlear implant.

The topics may change, but the core beliefs behind them do not. There will always be people who strongly believe in Deaf culture and those who oppose it. Changing anyone's opinion is a formidable task. The odds of getting someone to change his or her mind about deafness are about the same of getting someone to convert to a different religion.

If you adhere to any particular religious philosophy, chances are twenty years from now you will still have the same beliefs. Of course, there are exceptions. Every now and then, somebody goes through a major change and converts to a different religion. Usually, such a change involves some kind of profound life experience or epiphany.

Every year at Gallaudet University, you can see such an epiphany occurring for many new students. It happens when they suddenly discover that the deaf world has much more to offer than they'd ever imagined. Often, you will see them saying things like "Wow, I didn't know what I was missing!" and "It's great to meet other people who have been through the same thing I have." It is both empowering and enlightening.

Sometimes, it is the parents who are enlightened. MaryAnne Kowalczyk, for example, raised her deaf daughter from an oral perspective as instructed by medical professionals. She was absolutely convinced that she was doing the right thing and stood by her convictions for many years. But when her daughter inevitably discovered the deaf community, the changes were so positive and powerful that MaryAnne was inspired to found Parents for Deaf Awareness, an organization that promotes awareness of and involvement in the deaf world.

Nonetheless, for the majority of people, core beliefs are difficult if not impossible to change. If someone says "Sorry, but deafness is a nasty disability and it needs to be corrected by whatever medical means necessary," or "Deaf culture, deaf schmulture, you need to assimilate into the mainstream," then that person will most likely feel that way for a lifetime.

Face it: if you are deaf, the average hearing person probably views you as a defect. That's okay; people are entitled to their opinions. It's a free country. If my Uncle Louie in Idaho thinks I'm a moron because I don't wear a hearing aid, so be it. Your thoughts are free and they belong to you.

But when people in high places form opinions that are way off-kilter, that's when I start to become concerned. When politicians, teachers, administrators, and board members begin to adopt an extreme, one-size-fits-all mentality, the deaf community is in big trouble.

For the most part, extremist political views tend to favor the pathological. For example, I'm thinking of a former Human Services Director in North Carolina who equated sign language as "a form of abuse" and insinuated that cochlear implants and oralism are ideal for all deaf kids. But then again, it would be just as wrong if an ASL advocate insisted on ASL for mildly hard of hearing kids who do just fine with FM systems and hearing aids. One size simply does not fit all, and our nation's leaders must remember to respect diversity.

Every deaf organization, on local, statewide, and national levels, must do its best to educate the general community about deafness. People need to learn that there is more to deafness than just a disability, and that there is no single approach that works for every deaf person. Every option, every philosophy, every communication methodology needs to be made known. Too often, one has been touted as The Answer while another has been swept under the rug. Through proper education, this must stop. Ignorance needs to be replaced by awareness.

For this education to take place, we need to advertise ourselves big time. Sufficient exposure in the public eye is critical for ensuring that education and awareness takes place. At the 1998 NAD conference in San Antonio, for example, I was blown away by the fascinating, mind-boggling topics that opened my mind to new issues I wasn't aware of before. Yet something was missing. When I looked around, I noticed a glaring absence of hearing people. Hearing people who could have learned a thing or two about the wonderful world of Deaf culture.

Not that it was NAD's fault. They hold nothing back when it comes to advertising and promoting their national events. It's just that Deaf culture is too foreign, too far out in left field, for the average hearing person to comprehend. For organizations such as Self-Help for the Hard of Hearing (SHHH) and the Alexander Graham Bell Association for the Deaf, this is less of an issue because their philosophy is something the hearing world can easily understand and relate to. Not surprisingly, AG Bell and SHHH are successful at getting hearing people to attend their events. However, in Deaf culture, it's much harder. NAD and other culturally Deaf organizations have a perpetual uphill battle on their hands.

To overcome this, the culturally Deaf need to continuously enlighten the hearing world with the beauty and uniqueness of our culture. Opening our doors for the hearing to join our arts and cultural events is probably our most effective approach.

Certainly, we can teach, lecture, advocate, protest, rally, and debate until we are blue in the face, but nothing beats good old-fashioned fun and entertainment. I'm talking about enriching cultural events such as those hosted by Creative Access, an organization that wonderfully promotes the arts and culture in the deaf community.

Have you ever been to an open-captioned movie? A signed comedy, poetry, or dance performance

143

featuring deaf entertainers? A Broadway production interpreted into ASL? These are the types of events that Creative Access will host, and they are attended by both deaf and hearing people from all walks of life. It is at events like these that the average hearing person says, "Hey, deaf people are pretty neat. Their language and culture is so fascinating!" Boom, instant enlightenment. It's the best way to go.

In a nutshell, the most important message is probably this: however you chose to be deaf, celebrate it. Keep the door open and allow the hearing community to celebrate with you. The next generation of deaf people will thank you for it.

Intimate Moments

*I*ntimacy. Ugh! The very word makes average guys like me squirm. We'd rather spit, scratch, and hold burping contests instead of talking about our (gaaaack!) *feelings.* Oh, please. Guys just don't go there. Quit yapping and throw me another bag of potato chips, the game is on.

But as a deaf guy who's been left in the dark countless times, I have to suck in my pride and admit that, um, yeah, I do indeed, um, feel closer to certain people in my life because we can, um, (gaaaaaaack!!!) *communicate.*

To effectively communicate, you need to understand what your friends are saying. It doesn't take a rocket scientist, then, to figure out that for many deaf people, sign language is the key to communicating.

I bring this up because of a wry comment that caught my attention in a discussion group. Someone said that speech is most important because you need it to communicate with 99.9 percent of the population.

Good point, but what defines meaningful communication? There once was a time when I communicated reasonably well without sign language. Most of my hearing friends and classmates didn't sign, but at the time I thought we communicated just fine.

In retrospect, I realize that the best conversations, the ones of the "Whoa, that's deep" variety, occurred with the three or four friends who could sign.

At a recent workshop for deaf and hard of hearing children, one of the kids amazed me with a sobering confession. A clever twelve-year-old boy with excellent speech skills summed up his strategy for family events:

"I say hello," the boy said. "And then run!"

I asked him what he meant by "run." He explained that he would walk up to a group of hearing relatives, make polite conversation, and then move on to another group before the conversation went beyond "How are you," "How's the family," and "How's school."

He was an expert at lip-reading superficial conversation because he knew what to look for. But he also knew that if anyone changed the subject, he would have been like a deer frozen in headlights. So he took control, mastered the art of how-do-ya-do, and moved on. This kid definitely has a future in politics. He might not understand what people are saying but he sure knows how to work a room.

"But isn't that exhausting?" I asked, knowing all too well how I'd done the same thing when I was a kid.

"Yeah," said the boy, with several other kids nodding affirmatively. "Sometimes I sneak out and go to my room to play Nintendo for a while."

146

Do we call this effective communication? Not in my book. I call it Survival Skills of the Deaf and Hard of Hearing. We do what we do to get by. But getting back to my original point: what about intimate relationships?

I've said it before and I'll say it again: it wasn't until I found my niche in the deaf community that I learned how to really connect with people on a different level. Conversations suddenly became deeper, more meaningful.

Furthermore, with sign language it's easy to become immersed in group conversations. Years ago, when a group of hearing friends burst out in laughter, I would either ignore it and smile along like an idiot, or ask a trusted friend to repeat what was said. He would usually comply but it was not the same. I was playing catch-up. The moment itself was gone. Or, as the notoriously famous deaf quote goes, "Train gone."

You simply can't take those magic, spontaneous moments and recreate them. It just doesn't work when you say, "Hold it, everyone say that all over again slowly for the deaf guy." There's a natural flow to deep, intimate conversations. They just happen, and you're either fully involved in the moment or you're not. It's a spiritual aspect of our lives which is often overlooked but essential to all of us.

It may very well be true that 99.9 percent of the world uses speech (I don't know what the actual percentage is. I'm just humoring whoever came up with 99.9 percent). There's nothing wrong with deaf people using speech if they have the ability, nothing wrong with doing our part to meet hearing people halfway. And if not with speech, then with pen and paper, gesturing, interpreters, and so on. Whatever works.

But the fact of the matter is, it's the signing .1 percent of people that allows many of us to learn about ourselves and connect with others on a much deeper level. Certainly, the larger 99.9 percent is a huge rock that dwarfs the remaining .1 percent; but it is bigger only in terms of size. The remaining .1 percent is a finely cut diamond that has all the value and beauty in the world. I think we all deserve that .1 percent.

How Could it Happen?

*I*t's a story I've heard a million times. I've heard it from my parents, from many of their friends, and from senior members of various deaf organizations. It goes something like this:

> *"When my teacher caught me, I was sent to the principal's office."*
> *"My teacher hit me on the hands with a ruler."*
> *"I had to stand in the corner with my hands outstretched."*
> *"The principal pulled our pants down and whacked us on the butt with a paddle."*

What heinous crime had they committed? Nothing more than to dare to use sign language during school hours. For using the language that was most accessible to them, they got their butts whooped. No matter how many times I hear these stories, it never fails to elicit the same incredulous response:

> *How in the world could this be permitted to happen?*

149

Some of you may be rolling your eyes as you read this. Oh please, just let it go, you might think. That stuff happened more than thirty years ago. Deal with it and get a life. Those days are long gone.

Are they? I'm not so sure. What with the closings of deaf schools, the softening of the ADA, and the recent cochlear implant court case in Michigan (a social worker pushed for two deaf children temporarily under state custody to get implanted, against the wishes of their biological mother), there's always a gnawing fear in the back of my mind that people who claim to know what's best for us will once again send us back to the stone age.

It's my belief that in order to preserve the future, we must understand the past. That brings us back to my original question:

How in the world could this be permitted to happen?

It's a question I've started asking those who share their school horror stories from way back when. I had to ask because it still doesn't make sense. More specifically, I want to know: how could it go on for so long? Didn't anyone speak, er, sign up? I often wonder if anyone ever said, "Pardon me, teacher, but we'd get through this curriculum a heck of a lot faster if you would just sign." If anyone did indeed have the guts to say that, what happened to them?

Meanwhile, how could parents accept their kids getting whacked for using the language that came most naturally to them? Did the deaf community assertively fight for their rights or passively accept their fate?

150

I've asked a small number of people all of the above questions and I do have an interesting mix of answers. So far, here's what I have:

- Deaf people did speak up. The National Association of the Deaf, in fact, was founded to protect deaf professionals prior to the Milan Conference.

- Most of the deaf who spoke up for their rights were summarily ignored by the mainstream.

- There were also many deaf people who simply accepted it as "just the way things were."

- Lots of the aforementioned deaf people who "just accepted it" did so because there was no frame of reference (i.e. if they had a taste of just one class where the teacher signed, they never would have been able to go back to a class where signing was not permitted).

- There were deaf leaders who reluctantly kept their mouths shut out of fear of losing their jobs, which they needed to support their families.

I'm certain there's more to it than this. One helpful colleague suggested I look into Albert Ballin's *The Deaf Mute Howls,* originally published in 1930. Ballin makes such a passionate plea on behalf of sign language; apparently it fell on (pardon the pun) deaf ears. Regardless, the book has been resurrected by Gallaudet University Press, and I highly recommend it.

Again, I still don't have all the answers. How

come it took the many deaf people who were unhappy with oralism something like 90 years to finally get sign language into the classroom? How come, conversely, after a "voice off" ASL policy was recently implemented in some deaf schools, its vocal opponents got it dropped almost immediately?

Mind you, I do not have an issue with oralism itself. I have an issue with choices. Today, we pretty much have a wide range of choices to choose from, which is wonderful. But way back when, there was only one choice: stop signing, or have a nice little corporal visit with the principal. So tell me, how could it happen? I'd really like to know.

Editor's note: This article was originally published May 2003 in the National Association of the Deaf's Members Only *website.*

Super Phony on Spring Break

When we last left my infamous alter ego, the one and only Super Phony, he was still doing what he does best: looking like he knows what he's doing even when he doesn't have a blithering clue.

It takes an awful lot of effort to be the one deaf guy in a group of hearing people who don't sign. It requires a tremendous amount of patience, skill, strategy, and yes, deception.

Although he can slip back into his normal Clark Kent, uh, Mark Drolsbaugh personality in an ASL environment, Super Phony inevitably busts out of a telephone booth at the first hint of PWDS (people who don't sign).

Super Phony never rests in the presence of PWDS. It's a dirty job, but someone has to do it. Even during Spring Break in beautiful Cancun, Super Phony is just a misunderstood word away.

And in 1988, that's exactly what happened: Super Phony stole the show at Spring Break. Yes, around the same time some bona fide deaf heroes changed the world during the

Deaf President Now protest, Super Phony was causing mass confusion in Cancun.

While Gallaudetians were uniting for one of the biggest causes in deaf history, Super Phony was on a remote island with hearing students from Temple University. DPN certainly had his attention, so much that it would influence him to transfer to Gallaudet himself. But for the time being, there was other work to be done.

Namely, surviving Spring Break with two thousand rowdy hearing students. Super Phony only knew about five of them, but that didn't stop him. He went to all the parties, all the beach activities. Never mind that he rarely understood what people were saying. He was there, and he was making the most of it.

Making the most of it, when you're Super Phony, involves smiling a lot for no reason at all. It also involves saying "yes" to questions you don't understand. And this, of course, is what got Super Phony in yet another fine mess.

Our group had sailed on a party cruise to a private island just off Cancun and a wild celebration commenced. Little did Super Phony know what he was in for.

"Hey Mark," said Jennifer, a girl who was with the Temple University group. She pointed to a stage where a bunch of other students were lining up for an event.

"Would you like to blbshdks hdksju kssdib test?" I couldn't understand. I asked her to repeat.

"Would you like to blbshdks hdksju kssdib test?" Oh, boy. I was lost. I asked for one more repeat. Again, I could not understand.

By now, three of my hearing friends were standing

154

right behind her, giving me the thumbs up and vigorously nodding "Yes!" That was my cue. Time for SUPER PHONY! I smiled and said yes.

Next thing I knew, Jennifer grabbed my hand and dragged me towards the stage. There were about ten other couples already there and an emcee was running the show. Having watched a lot of MTV, I figured this was one of those rowdy Spring Break competitions where you do a lot of stupid but harmless stuff. Maybe it was a dirty dancing contest. Perhaps some goofy event involving water balloons, food fights, relay races, or even a burping contest. Whatever it was, I was up for it. Or was I?

Never in a million years would I have been able to guess what was going to happen next. I stood onstage like a clueless moron for five minutes as the emcee worked the crowd. Then finally, it was show time. The emcee pointed at those of us onstage and yelled, "Go!"

All of a sudden, everyone started smooching. I mean, really, really, making out. Couples were playing tongue hockey. Everyone was all hot and heavy. Grinding, groping, licking and slurping. Oh, no. Super Phony was trapped... in a kissing contest!

Super Phony stood there, horrified. He could see his pals in the first row. They were pointing at him and howling with laughter. He glanced at Jennifer, who wasn't exactly Cindy Crawford. He didn't even know her until ten minutes ago.

Wincing, Super Phony puckered up. Jennifer grabbed him in a bear hug and planted a wet one on his lips. But Super Phony was in a total state of shock and he reacted like a passionless rag doll. Super Phony and his kissing bandit were immediately voted off stage as the lamest couple.

"Ptooie!" I sputtered, wiping my lips. "I can't believe I got suckered into that." My buddies laughed so hard, tears were streaming down their faces.

But that's cool. If anything, Super Phony is a good sport. And he never makes the same mistake twice.

Then, suddenly, a voice blared over the speakers: "Attention, Spring Breakers, attention... mooning contest at Dock Four, line up now..."

It Was Worth It

When I wrote and published my first book *Deaf Again*, it was one of the hardest things I ever did in my life. Normally, writing a book and having it published is the thrill of a lifetime. But this book was a bit too personal. This was about my family, all the good stuff and the bad stuff. Mostly good stuff, but the bad stuff was brutally honest. Like many other deaf people with hearing relatives, I often find myself twiddling my thumbs at the dinner table. It can be a bummer. So I wrote about it.

When the first shipment of books was fresh off the press, however, I froze in my tracks. I couldn't go through with it. Every worse-case scenario flashed through my mind. My family was either going to have their feelings hurt or they were going to be mad as hell. Or both. They would disown me and I would move to a remote cabin somewhere in Switzerland.

After much soul-searching, I decided to go for it with *Deaf Again*. If I was guilty of anything, it was of telling the truth. Truth that needed to be heard. My biggest reinforcement came from

157

Lisa Bain, an accomplished writer who has published three books of her own. When I expressed my concern that family members might feel bad about certain deaf issues, she smiled knowingly. Then in her own polite, thoughtful way, she asked:

"Don't you think they already know?"

She was right. They did know. It was never an issue of knowing about deafness. It was about coping with deafness. There were no answers for my family until they read the book. Immediately, the changes were obvious.

During a small get-together with hearing friends and relatives, my hearing grandmother caught me struggling to keep up with a conversation. She saw me straining to read lips, asking for clarification, and finally just nodding off when it got too frustrating. Grandmom turned to my mother and said something that took her by surprise.

"He doesn't understand a word, does he?"

At last! She finally understood. She saw my world for what it really was. So much, in fact, that for the next major family gathering she made arrangements for a sign language interpreter. Pah! What followed was a major breakthrough.

Three weeks later, we were together again; only this time, we had an interpreter. It was nirvana. Dinner table conversation was no longer a bore. Grandmom told a story about how her mother used to keep live fish in the bathtub before preparing them for dinner. My uncle and two other relatives were in a heavy debate about religious pluralism. I watched with fascination. A whole new world had opened. These strangers at the dinner table had suddenly transformed into very interesting people!

It didn't matter if the deaf relatives were actively

involved in the conversation or not. Sometimes we jumped in; sometimes we just sat back and enjoyed the show. With the interpreter, we had a new set of ears that let us know what was going on at all times. There was no boredom whatsoever.

The real kicker was a conversation with my cousin Eleanor. A pleasant young woman, Eleanor has always been an interesting person. However, her speech pattern, for whatever reason, has always been difficult for me to follow. I never realized it until just then, but I had always manipulated our conversations in such a way that it never went beyond the superficial. For if we had ever jumped to a brand new topic I would not have been able to keep up. It's much easier to lip-read when you know the conversation will stick to "How's the family" and "How's the job."

With the interpreter, though, we reached new heights. During the discussion on religious issues I was surprised to find myself agreeing with Eleanor several times. From a philosophical standpoint we were practically twins. Only then, after all these years, did I realize this. To top it off, I also discovered she takes an Aikido class and shares a similar interest in the martial arts. I've been a martial arts nut for several years yet never had such a discussion with Eleanor. I had no idea she was into the same thing. We wound up having a great talk, sharing notes about our respective martial arts styles. All of this thanks to the interpreter.

When the evening drew to a close, I checked my watch and did a double take. It was 10:30 pm. Under the usual circumstances (no interpreter and plenty of boredom) I would have been out of there by 7:30. This time, however, I stayed for the whole duration and got to know my family on an entirely different level. So looking back on *Deaf Again...* yes, it was deafinitely worth it.

159

You Deaf People

*F*or years, I've put audiences all over the nation to sleep with my incoherent presentation on deaf awareness. A pinch of psychobabble here, a touch of Eastern philosophy there, and snoring audiences everywhere.

But at a recent workshop, I decided to take a walk on the wild side. Rather than drone on with pre-planned, pre-fab material, I tossed my notes aside and opened the floor for many hearing parents of deaf children. The questions and resulting discussions were quite insightful, yet something was still missing. Everyone was trying too hard to be politically correct. Nice, yes, but we lacked an "edge."

No problem. Prior to a break in the workshop, I passed out pieces of paper with instructions to write down any questions or comments. No topic was off-limits. Furthermore, it was anonymous. No names were to be used and thus we could easily address *Everything You Wanted to Know About Deafness But Were Afraid to Ask.* In the shadow of anonymity, people tend to be braver and more likely to say

160

what's really on their minds.

And during the intermission, one of the written questions jumped right out and smacked me in the face:

"*What is it with you deaf people,*" the note began. "*Why are you always so angry about the cochlear implant? What is it about Deaf culture that makes you have a chip on your shoulder when the hearing world is trying to help you?*" Needless to say, I had found my edge.

The question was read out loud to the parents and I noticed everyone shifting forward in their seats. Ah, finally I had their undivided attention. Okay, so it took a *Jerry Springer* approach. But I had their attention. Controversy sells, baby.

Yes, we tactfully dealt with the cochlear implant issue, discussing in depth why some people like it and some don't. We also discussed the importance of avoiding stereotypes because opinions on the implant vary both within and outside the deaf community.

The parents were very satisfied with the discussion and we moved on to other equally challenging topics: what to do when hearing relatives won't learn sign language, job opportunities for deaf people in the 21st century, literacy issues, and more. It was a smashing success.

On the flight home, however, something gnawed at me. I loved all of the questions, no matter how crazy or controversial—but three words stuck out like a sore thumb: *you deaf people.*

I did not interpret the wording as derogatory— in fact, I appreciate how the person who wrote it was being up front with her feelings. What really concerned me, instead, was the way this person distanced herself from the deaf. In other words: what is it with *you* people, *you* Deaf culture types? What's the matter with *you*? Why can't *you* see that *I'm* doing what *I* believe is best for *you*?

It was a disturbing, gaping chasm of separateness. It was disturbing because ultimately, we are all in this together. Let's take a look at this phenomenon and see if, somehow, there is hope for repairing the gap.

First and foremost, we must put ourselves in parents' shoes. We all know how traumatic it is when hearing parents first discover their child is deaf. It is a tremendous shock, and this is only the beginning.

After the initial blow that comes with diagnosis of a child's hearing loss, parents are soon confronted with another challenge. They are besieged with advice from a number of professionals, many of them pushing extreme views that favor one methodology over another. In most cases it will be doctors or audiologists pushing for audist approaches such as speech therapy, hearing aids, and cochlear implants. Some of these experts will even warn the parents not to expose their deaf children to sign language or Deaf culture.

This is where the cavalry comes to the rescue, right? The deaf community, after all, can tell parents how wonderful ASL and Deaf culture happen to be. That'll set everything straight, won't it?

Nope. On the contrary, if we're not careful, we can make everything even worse. When a strong ASL/Deaf culture advocate tells parents that everything the doctors said was all hooey, we now have confused parents stuck in the middle of two extremes.

On top of that, our wonderful world of ASL and Deaf culture is completely foreign to most hearing parents; it's like we're from another planet. And we're telling these parents that their kids are better off interacting with a different group of people who use a different language? *Of course* they don't like it, and they no longer know who to believe anymore.

Sadly, we often become the straw that breaks the camel's back. On more than one occasion I've seen parents driven away by well-meaning but overzealous people in the deaf community. The parents say, "Okay, that's it. You can't tell me how to raise my child. I'm not gonna take it anymore." Who can blame them?

Further compounding the problem is the all-too-prevalent either/or mentality. Few people objectively provide parents with enough information to be able to choose from the varying options that match their child's strengths. It's an option, for example, to wear a hearing aid *and* use sign language.

As a result of being bombarded with extreme viewpoints, parents often wind up wrestling with very difficult choices. Influenced by the either/or mentality, they usually choose this methodology over that methodology without incorporating the best of whatever each one has to offer.

Consequently, when parents finally make a choice, they may move on with it—but deep down, they will always question themselves: *Are we doing the right thing?* To constantly second-guess your decision is tantamount to inviting a nervous breakdown. You can't do it. You need to have your choices justified, validated somehow.

So, whenever anyone chooses one methodology over another, to avoid any further mental anguish that person may go out of his or her way to disparage the other methodology. To justify that one made the right decision, to eliminate all nagging doubt, one feels better by distancing him or herself from those who take a different approach. And now we understand why that lady referred to me and my friends as *you deaf people*.

There are two answers to this predicament that come to mind. The first one is that all organizations should take it as an ethical and professional responsibility to provide parents with as much information as possible. Information is power, and with children, all power rightfully belongs to the parents. If an organization deliberately withholds information or constantly criticizes those who do things differently, then that organization is contributing to the massive mind-screwing of parents everywhere.

The other answer is to implore parents and people in general to be more open-minded, and to be willing to walk a mile in someone else's shoes before passing judgment. We have to remember that *every* group, race, religion, and organization has its share of good apples and bad apples.

If I may make a martial arts analogy, I have been involved in three different martial arts styles for almost fifteen years. My experience in the martial arts has been overwhelmingly positive. But you know what? I've seen my fair share of nuts out there. For every ten honorable martial artists, there's one demented psychopath who's in it for all the wrong reasons. Nonetheless, you don't see me quitting and saying *bah, you martial arts types*.

Likewise, do not give up on any aspect of the deaf community. Instead, strive to understand, strive to learn what works for you and your child, and make the most of it. And, above all, keep an open mind.

Editor's note: In addition to originally appearing in the November 2000 Silent News, *this article was also published in the Summer/Fall 2001 issue of* Kaleidoscope.